POEMS FOR Courage

Stories to Inspire and Guide

K.S. DWYER

outskirts
press

Poems for Courage
Stories to Inspire and Guide
All Rights Reserved.
Copyright © 2024 K.S. Dwyer
v24.0 r1.3

This is a work of allegories and non-fiction. The opinions expressed in this manuscript are solely the opinions of the author and do not represent the opinions or thoughts of the publisher. The author has represented and warranted full ownership and/or legal right to publish all the materials in this book.

This book may not be reproduced, transmitted, or stored in whole or in part by any means, including graphic, electronic, or mechanical without the express written consent of the publisher except in the case of brief quotations embodied in critical articles and reviews.

Outskirts Press, Inc.
http://www.outskirtspress.com

ISBN: 978-1-9772-6298-1

Cover Photo © 2024 www.gettyimages.com. All rights reserved - used with permission.

Outskirts Press and the "OP" logo are trademarks belonging to Outskirts Press, Inc.

PRINTED IN THE UNITED STATES OF AMERICA

Praise for
Poems for Courage

"Through his heartfelt poetry and poetic stories – whether experienced firsthand or shared with him by others – and by encouraging our own written reflections, K.S. Dwyer challenges us to be mindful of a higher perspective, to turn misfortune into fortune, and to know gratitude and compassion. As he writes in 'Overcoming the Odds,' 'Our circumstances do not define who we are and who we become, but can propel each of us where we are meant to be.'"
- *David Tate, PhD*

"No matter the darkness or difficulties presented in life, to read *Poems for Courage* is to feel that we are not alone in the human experience. This collection encourages us to see beyond oneself when possible, promoting even greater healing."
- *Candice Fry, MA, LCSW, BSP*

"This collection of anthologies and vignettes is a powerful source of inspiration, engaging the reader and evoking warm, positive, and optimistic feelings."
- *Dwight Williams, Adjunct Professor, Doctorate*

"K.S. Dwyer writes with inspiration and it shows. His commitment to giving hope and courage to all people permeates every word of *Poems for Courage*."
- *Brielle C. Meredith, Board of Directors - Mona Lisa Foundation*

"This collection is far reaching and wide in experiences. Each gem delivers a nugget to touch the individual on a personal level. Indeed, there is something for everybody waiting to be discovered.

I believe that as humans, we live in a world of the physical, the cognitive, and the spiritual. To stay in balance from day to day, we need to nourish each of these areas. *Poems for Courage* provides access to the cognitive and spiritual appetites that need feeding on a daily basis."

- *Bart Andrus, M.S. ED, Head Coach Philadelphia Stars, United States Football League, former NFL coach*

"This book will pull you through the depths of a dark time. Remind you of your life's purpose. Help you to take steps forward on your life path. Coming back to the heart when the brain takes over. If you're struggling or just looking to grow, this book is for you. "

- *Emily Brough, Yoga Instructor, Licensed Massage Therapist, Rock Climber, Outdoor Guide*

"To read this book is to embrace the human experience and to be inspired to have courage in the pursuit of finding others to lift and love."

- *Shanon Brooks, PhD*

*"Nothing in life is more exciting and rewarding than the sudden flash of insight that leaves you a changed person,
not only changed, but for the better."*
— *Arthur Gordon*

"The most difficult thing is the decision to act, the rest is merely tenacity."
— *Amelia Earhart*

"Sometimes in this life, in order to become the person we are meant to be, we need to practice forgiveness and letting go."
— *K.S. Dwyer*

"It's not enough to have love, you must also have gratitude. Love is the door to fulfillment and happiness but gratitude is the key that unlocks that door."
— *Kristen Weber*

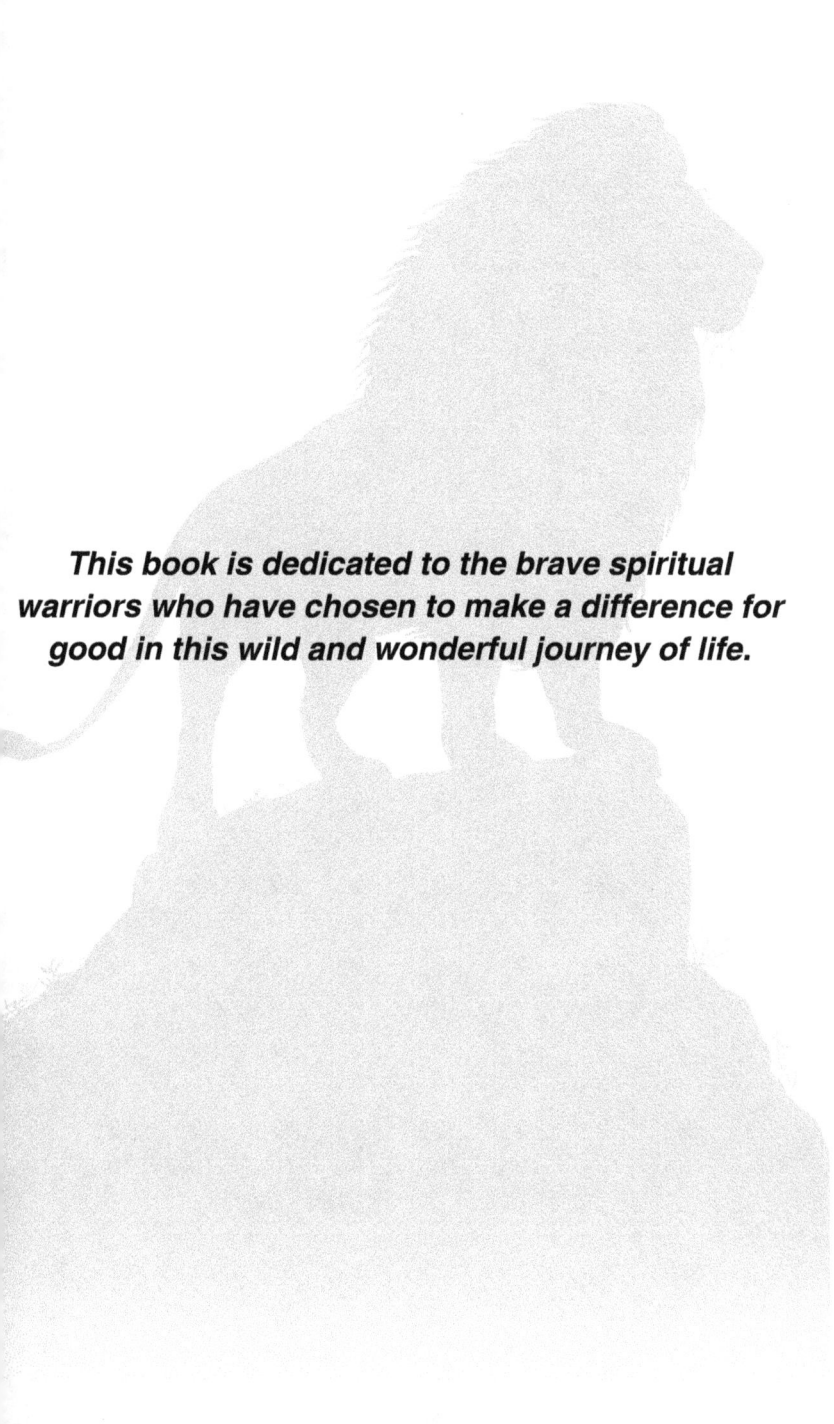

This book is dedicated to the brave spiritual warriors who have chosen to make a difference for good in this wild and wonderful journey of life.

Table of Contents

Foreword i
Prologue: A Warrior's Soul Calls From Within v
1. A Taste of Coastal Bliss 1
2. God's Willing Hand 5
3. Seeds of Greatness 12
4. A Ray of Hope 16
5. I Do See 20
6. A Mother's Loving Prayer 24
7. I Am 29
8. Answering the Call 35
9. Top of the Mountain 39
10. It Will Be All Right 49
11. The Gift of Freedom 54
12. In the Moment 57
13. On the Ropes 60
14. Of the Heart 66
15. True Friendship 70
16. Duty to Lift Up 74
17. Inner Strength 79
18. By My Side 83
19. Take That First Step 87
20. It Matters to Me 93
21. Rekindle Your Dreams 97
22. Courage to Stand 102
23. We All Matter 106
24. Here With Me 110
25. A Time to Rise Up 116
26. Opportunity in Adversity 122

27. Nurtured By Nature	127
28. More Valuable Than Gold	131
29. Those Who Believe	136
30. Your Truth	142
31. Angels' Landing	145
32. Breaking the Chains	153
33. Blue Coast Courage	157
34. The Path of Giants	172
35. You Have Purpose	176
36. Inspirational Drive	181
37. Beyond the Hunger	189
38. In Honor Of	196
39. Forty-five Cents	203
40. Why Not You?	210
41. In the Service of Others	215
42. A Mother's Love	221
43. Your Mind	226
44. From the Ashes	232
45. Ship of Dreams	238
46. Overcoming the Odds	245
47. When Comes A Call	251
48. Active Faith	255
49. The Other Side	261
50. There is a Season	269
51. Righteous Among Nations	275
52. On Bended Knee	281
Afterword	287
Acknowledgments	291
About the Author	293
Sources	295

Foreword

It has been a challenging few years to be a human. A global pandemic, rising inflation, geopolitical instability, and increasing worries about climate change are ever-present concerns that can often seem suffocating in their breadth and width. But regardless of the time or the year, there will always be different seasons to our life: challenge, success, difficulty, and achievement. It's a constant cycle. One can be forgiven for feeling like each day is an exercise not in thriving, but in endurance; simply getting to the end of the day in one piece is an accomplishment. And yet, day after day, week after week, month after month, if we're living just to get by, we'll soon find that something is missing.

Many people have conducted interviews with hospice patients during their end of life care about their biggest regrets. Inc.com has run several of these pieces.[1] The answers people give are telling. "I wish I'd spent more time with the people I love," "I wish I'd cared less about what other people thought," "I wish I'd worked less," etc. All of these answers have one thing in common: they take courage. We don't often think of spending more time with our family as a courageous act, but that is exactly what it is. It takes courage to set aside

---

1 https://www.inc.com/lolly-daskal/12-things-people-regret-the-most-before-they-die.html

the work, the day to day drudgery and logistics to be fully present with a parent, child, or partner. Likewise, it takes courage to be confident enough in oneself to stop caring what others think or letting those opinions control you. Living our life so that we minimize our regrets and are free to live the full measure of our creation takes true courage.

It also takes great courage to face things head on. Difficult diagnoses, disappointments, heartbreak, and slights all require us to humble ourselves, find strength, and do what must be done. Knowing that we already have the capacity to face what lies ahead takes courage as well.

Finally, it takes immense amounts of courage to let go. Courage is, according to the book, *Letting Go: The Pathway to Surrender* by David R. Hawkins, MD, PhD[2], an energy; it is an energy that says "I can do it." It is determined, excited about life, productive, independent, and self-empowered."

At its root, the word courage comes from the *French word, "coeur" which means "heart."* Courage is a matter of the heart

This acknowledgement of the heart and this self-empowerment are the goals of K.S. Dwyer's new collection of poems and poetic stories, *Poems for Courage*. Building on the momentum of his previous

---

[2] Hawkins, David R. *Letting Go: The Pathway to Surrender*, Veritas, 2013

collection, *Poetry for Peace*, *Poems for Courage* aims to encourage readers to identify areas in their lives where they must be courageous – and to celebrate those moments with reflection and gratitude. Designed as an interactive book for reflection interspersed with poetic stories, *Poems for Courage* emboldens readers to consider the stories of others who have faced times of challenge and who have found within themselves the courage to carry on and to create joy.

While this world may be one of often overwhelming difficulty and challenge, carving out moments of peace and appreciation and working to minimize our regrets is a truly courageous act. *Poems for Courage* is meant as a guide, a valuable roadmap to stoke the courage within and to seek out moments of beauty and gratitude, so that we may fully appreciate those relationships and endeavors we have in our lives.

After each poem or poetic story, space is provided to reflect upon its application to you. K.S. encourages you to do so throughout by writing about:

1. Any valuable **insights** you have gained;
2. Any **actions** you feel inspired to take;
3. Any **letting go** (forgiving or letting go of grief) needed; and/or
4. Any **gratitude** or **love** you feel compelled to express.

It takes courage to reflect upon and articulate about those things of which we become aware. To do so can significantly support our emotional and physical health[3] and can help cultivate wisdom, determination, freedom, love, gratitude, and – at the root of them all – courage.

---

[3] Pennebaker, James W. *Opening Up: The Healing Power of Expressing Emotions*, 2nd Ed. 1997.

Prologue: A Warrior's Soul Calls From Within

There came a stunning celestial morning, full of shimmering hues. It was awash in the most beautiful colors, those only angels and heavenly beings had seen. It could only be described as an ethereal word. Shimmering, sapphire blues, glimmering, yellow golds, blindingly bright whites. Even the sun was overjoyed.

Then, there came a voice. Peaceful, but strong. So calm, yet so wise. Through the heavens it resounded. "Angels, find me a warrior. Someone with the courage to know they can draw on strength beyond themselves. Someone with the gift of humility, who will be forever learning. This person needs the heart, the spirit, the soul of a champion. They need the perspective and vision to see beyond every trial, setback, and heartache. They need to see beyond the loss. They must be resilient, and able to recognize their great gifts. These talents they possess must be shared with others as they help fellow people increase their own talents and gifts. This person must be willing to accept help from others, as well as to give help when it is needed. They must help others to rise above, to see the light in a nighttime of darkness. To see the path when all roads seem blocked. To hear the answer when nothing but silence can be heard. When courage is difficult to come by, this person must be able to dig down deep, find their grit and fortitude, and do what must be done.

"This person will not live a common life. They will experience strength and miracles that will take their breath away. Their courage will grow over time, adding to their wisdom, which will become a wellspring as they continue to search for knowledge and drink from the flowing waters therein. They will make a difference for good, forever fulfilling the measure of their creation. They will leave a legacy for those who follow in their footsteps. When they return, my son and I, with the celestial host, knowing all of the world's challenges, will say, 'Well done, my true courageous and spiritual warrior. You made each day count. You learned, you grew, you helped others. You continually found the courage to rise.'"

Then the voice asked if we had a person of such faith and gifts.

"Yes. We have. They are right here, reading or listening to these words. They are with us now."

It has always been you!

1

A Taste of Coastal Bliss

Sipping chocolate by the sea.
What kind? You say.
Warm as day.
Sipping chocolate by the sea
with you in the evening is
where I want to be.[1]

With my arm around you,
look up at the sky.
See the many stars.
Reach up and grab one
Don't ask why.

How does it feel to have
the cool ocean air
flow across the sand
and curl your hair?

Sipping hot chocolate is [2]
where I want to be.
Look into my eyes and
soon you will see.

That sipping hot chocolate
by the sea
is a perfect beginning
for you and me.

Hold my hand and let
me say,
"Oh how I love you."
What a perfect way to spend
this beautiful day.

I find time to breathe, ponder, and reflect on

_____
_____
_____
_____
_____
_____
_____
_____
_____
_____
_____
_____

*I find time for love, joy, and
take time to write about*

_____
_____
_____
_____
_____
_____
_____
_____
_____
_____
_____
_____

*I take time to forgive and
release and write about*

_____
_____
_____
_____
_____
_____
_____
_____
_____
_____
_____

*I take time to respect and prioritize
my endeavors and write about*

_____
_____
_____
_____
_____
_____
_____
_____
_____
_____
_____
_____

2
God's Willing Hand

Looking into her strong, clear
eyes, the young, newly enlisted
airman took her into his arms.
First an affectionate hug,
then a passionate kiss.
With tears in his voice,
he said, "I love you."
"Yes," she replied. "I love you too."

Serving his country, protecting
families, defending freedom
he felt called to do.[3]

Arriving in England,
he was assigned to a flight crew of ten.
Their motto: "Aim high, fly, fight, win."
If they survived the mission,
then back to the skies in a
B-17 bomber, the Flying Fortress[4]
would do it all again.
In the throes of World War II
casualties were historically high.

Fighting against evil,
tyranny, oppression, and genocide.
The young airman and crew
became warriors of the skies.

On their thirty-fifth mission
the squadron, crew, and plane
found themselves in turbulent
ice, wind, clouds, and flak,
facing heavy enemy attack.

Swarms of enemy fighters
continued to release a barrage
of bullets and cannon fire.

Airman, defending, continuing
to attack.
Incredibly outnumbered
fire, flames, and smoke
filling their plane.
A hail of bullets and cannon
fire riddled their fortress
like heavy rain.
Their fortress now bending,
melting, coming apart.
Each airman, with a quick
glance
heard the Captain's
words:

"Parachutes on. Bail out!
It's our only chance!"

They found themselves in
freezing winds, floating
in the skies.
Who would survive?
Who would die?

The airmen hit
the hard, frozen land
and found themselves
surrounded
by enemy soldiers
with guns in hand.

Taking prisoners is how
the story goes.
All the inhumane
conditions and
barbaric ways.
Many back in their homeland
continued to pray.
For those missing in action.
For those who mourn.
For the POWs.
A mission,
a sojourn.

The young airman who had
so affectionately embraced
then passionately kissed his
loving wife goodbye,
finding himself on forced death marches
where many did die.

After enduring much cold,
hungry, and exhausted
with little end in sight,
he felt he could not go any further.
He was losing his fight.

But he knew if he stopped,
he would be beat or shot.

Then, looking up, he saw the
beautiful spiritual countenance[5]
of his wife,
her arms wide open,
her eyes filled with strength.
In his heart and mind
he heard her say, "Come on, Bill.
You can do it."
He finished the march that day.[6]

Soon the war would come
to an end.
Liberated and on a plane,

he began to realize
as most spiritual warriors do,
that we are never alone.

If we have faith, hope, and
courage, we will find
strength beyond our own.

Many of honor, of valor
have fought.
A price they paid.
Our freedom, our liberty sought.[7]

Freedom fighters and spiritual
warriors know,
with perseverance and grit,
"You can do it."

I find time to breathe, ponder, and reflect on

_____
_____
_____
_____
_____
_____
_____
_____
_____
_____
_____
_____

*I find time for love, joy, and
take time to write about*

_____
_____
_____
_____
_____
_____
_____
_____
_____
_____
_____
_____

*I take time to forgive and
release and write about*

_____
_____
_____
_____
_____
_____
_____
_____
_____
_____

*I take time to respect and prioritize
my endeavors and write about*

_____
_____
_____
_____
_____
_____
_____
_____
_____
_____

3
Seeds of Greatness

In the darkest of nights
through the roughest storms of life,
know this: it will be all right.

Some of the greatest challenges
are given to God's strongest spiritual warriors.

All storms plant innumerable seeds.
Some bring courage.
Some strength beyond your own.
Some, the additional wisdom to succeed.

You are here to make a difference.[8]
You are a warrior.
When on bended knee,
you plead.
Only to hear, "I am with you."

As the storm clouds begin to dissipate
others come to help.
They did not hesitate.[9]

So you may ask why
you hear the words
"You are a child of the most high."

Through the fire, the flames with
embers so bright,
come follow me as we share the light.

I find time to breathe, ponder, and reflect on

_____
_____
_____
_____
_____
_____
_____
_____
_____
_____
_____
_____

*I find time for love, joy, and
take time to write about*

_____
_____
_____
_____
_____
_____
_____
_____
_____
_____
_____
_____

*I take time to forgive and
release and write about*

_____
_____
_____
_____
_____
_____
_____
_____
_____
_____

*I take time to respect and prioritize
my endeavors and write about*

_____
_____
_____
_____
_____
_____
_____
_____
_____
_____
_____

4
A Ray of Hope

Nestled by the golden yellow aspens
next to the red and orange maples
was a modest home.
A window open to hear the
ripples of the nearby brook.

The keeper would feed the hungry.
Help the children learn to fish.
He would share his food, his dish. [10]

He loved sunrises and the sunsets.
For he knew hunger, he knew pain.
He believed there was music in the rain.

A cup of warmth in the morning.
Never afraid to share a plate at night.
Letting each know it would be all right.
You see he was a veteran.
He had put his life on the line.
Through a series of unfortunate events,
over seventy percent of his body burned.
But the giver of Hope, a title he earned. [11]

Although, burned, broken, and bruised,
   faith and fortitude he did stand.
    A wellspring of Hope,
  an extension of the Master's hands.

I find time to breathe, ponder, and reflect on

_____
_____
_____
_____
_____
_____
_____
_____
_____
_____
_____
_____

*I find time for love, joy, and
take time to write about*

_____
_____
_____
_____
_____
_____
_____
_____
_____
_____
_____
_____

*I take time to forgive and
release and write about*

_____

_____

_____

_____

_____

_____

_____

_____

_____

_____

*I take time to respect and prioritize
my endeavors and write about*

_____

_____

_____

_____

_____

_____

_____

_____

_____

_____

5
I Do See

Having a sense of purpose
can bring great joy.
Each day millions go
without food or clean water.
You are enough.
You can make a difference.[12]

Each night many sleep in
cars or on the streets
for they have not a place
to call home.

You are a spiritual warrior.
You have a great purpose.
You can feed with food.
You can house with resources.
You can feed with a kind word.

As the gladiators of old were
called forth to fight,
you have been called to
walk the path of light
to share your gifts
to share your insight.[13]

Don't waste time fighting
for this life is short.
Define your goals.
Don't sweat the small stuff.
Find gratitude.
For you really are
absolutely enough.

Take time to connect with
nature.
Spend time on
that which really matters.

Meditate and pray for purpose,
wisdom, and focus.
In doing so,
you will be able to live
a full life
while helping and serving
others.
After all, what really matters? Love,
relationships, kindness, caring for others.

Stop caring what other's think.
Enjoy the full measure of your creation.
Let your warrior's path be
so you can say, "I do see!"

I find time to breathe, ponder, and reflect on

_____
_____
_____
_____
_____
_____
_____
_____
_____
_____
_____
_____

*I find time for love, joy, and
take time to write about*

_____
_____
_____
_____
_____
_____
_____
_____
_____
_____
_____
_____

*I take time to forgive and
release and write about*

_____
_____
_____
_____
_____
_____
_____
_____
_____
_____

*I take time to respect and prioritize
my endeavors and write about*

_____
_____
_____
_____
_____
_____
_____
_____
_____
_____
_____

6
A Mother's Loving Prayer

Tears of a mother fall
like drops of rain.
As she can only imagine
her child's pain.[14]

She has not, but the ability
to pray.
As she searched for food
this day.

She bows her head mostly
from shame.
Then on bended knee the
tears begin to flow.

A heartfelt prayer only the
Angels in heaven and He knows.
This night has come and gone.
The child now sleeps.
While all night long, the mother weeps.
Sunshine now breaks open
the day.[15]

Will she or they have the
strength to make it another
day?

A knock at the door, she
moves to see who is there.
A stranger's face, he speaks
with no despair.

I could not sleep, the
stranger says.[16]
So he meditated and prayed
throughout the night.

Then a prompting let him
know,
"Just what to to do,
What to say."

The stranger then motioned
for others to come.
This they did.
What a tidy sum.

Bringing in food, clothing,
some money, and toys.
For with the spirit of giving and grace,
their eyes filled with tears.
The stranger then asked

if that would help?
"Yes," she replied, "what might
I do?"
"Send a prayer to another.
Bless them, as I have you."

When she looked up to say she would,
the stranger was gone, so she
closed the door
and knelt as the
words came out.
She understood.

A stranger in her midst
had come.
But not a stranger to her now.[17]

Her child, now content.
Yes, he was heaven sent.

Mother's prayer can change the day.
Mother's prayer can make a way.
Mother's prayer can protect.
Mother's prayer to direct.

I find time to breathe, ponder, and reflect on

_____
_____
_____
_____
_____
_____
_____
_____
_____
_____
_____

*I find time for love, joy, and
take time to write about*

_____
_____
_____
_____
_____
_____
_____
_____
_____
_____

*I take time to forgive and
release and write about*

_____
_____
_____
_____
_____
_____
_____
_____
_____
_____
_____

*I take time to respect and prioritize
my endeavors and write about*

_____
_____
_____
_____
_____
_____
_____
_____
_____
_____
_____
_____

7
I Am

I am in the golden blue
hues of the rising sun.
I am in the basking
warmth of the morning rays.

Though the end of my earthly
days did arrive,
I walk with you in spirit.
For in your heart and memories,[18]
I am alive

Look for me in the beauty of
the blue and red rose.
Let the softness
of the petal touch your
face.
Our memories are
eternal
never to
erase.
I am in the cooing of
a dove.

A soaring eagle's whispering
wind.
Of my blessings, kindness
and love without end,
I will send.

In the crystal blue waves you
will see my eyes.
In the setting of the sun.
you will find my
peace.

In your favorite song,
you will hear me.
In the quiet of the
moment,
you will feel me.
In the smile of
greatness, I will be.

I am in the gathering of many,
yet I visit the one
of my work.
Like the masterpiece
of the artist,
we are
never done.
I am in the silence
of the deepest forest,

the tallest trees.
Take time to visit
with joy
on bended knee.
A little meditation is where I will be.

I am the strength
that carries you
in the toughest
of times.

I am the helping hand.
Hear me in the
bluebirds' song.
See me in the
miracle of the
hummingbird's flight.

I am with you in the
darkest night.
As you walk this path
we call life.
I will always
guide you to
the light.
I am in you.
You are in my heart.
I promise to look out
for you.

Now as one of your
Angels
out of love,
I am bound.
This is not goodbye[19]
or the end.
Just another chapter
together.
So let's begin.

I am the love
you have felt today.
You are the priceless
treasures in
so many ways.
Never forget
you are
never alone.
You are everything to
me.
Take time
to find the
sea.
Just take a
moment.
Just be.
Just see.

I am with you.

I find time to breathe, ponder, and reflect on

_____
_____
_____
_____
_____
_____
_____
_____
_____
_____
_____

*I find time for love, joy, and
take time to write about*

_____
_____
_____
_____
_____
_____
_____
_____
_____
_____
_____

*I take time to forgive and
release and write about*

_____
_____
_____
_____
_____
_____
_____
_____
_____
_____
_____

*I take time to respect and prioritize
my endeavors and write about*

_____
_____
_____
_____
_____
_____
_____
_____
_____
_____
_____
_____

8
Answering the Call

It was not a lot that I
had to give.

No it was not money or
other possessions.

It was heartfelt.
It was directed.
I picked up the phone.
I made the call.

I had put it off most of the day.
Due to the fact that I was not
sure what to say.[20]

We had been in a disagreement
for quite a while.

I only said, "Hello, I have felt
impressed to call you."
I did not say much after that.
Other than an occasional, "Yes, I understand."[21]

I guess he had spoken
for quite some time, but as indicated,
I listened most of the time.
He could only see the darkness.
With each word, I could feel his pain.
He asked for a moment to wipe his tears.
Then thanked me for my listening ears.

As the conversation drew to a
close, there was much appreciation
offered to me.
I felt I had not been the
one so deserving.

The next day, I received a
call.
My dear friend, whom I spoke
with a little and listened to a lot
had decided to stay
and not end it all.

Listening is another form of
feeding.
This is something, we are all needing.

What if I had not made
the call?
Listen we shall, listen to all.

I find time to breathe, ponder, and reflect on

_____
_____
_____
_____
_____
_____
_____
_____
_____
_____
_____
_____

*I find time for love, joy, and
take time to write about*

_____
_____
_____
_____
_____
_____
_____
_____
_____
_____

*I take time to forgive and
release and write about*

_____
_____
_____
_____
_____
_____
_____
_____
_____
_____
_____

*I take time to respect and prioritize
my endeavors and write about*

_____
_____
_____
_____
_____
_____
_____
_____
_____
_____
_____
_____

9

Top of the Mountain

During the three-hour hike
to the top of the mountain,
he had made a series
of rationalizations about why
this would be the end of
his days on this earth.

He had become his own judge
and jury.
The sentence for his actions[22]
would be a quick jump.
In his mind, it was the last time
he would fall short.

Such a young age to be
full of such disappointment,
and such rage.
With each step closer
to the top, he
would set himself free
of this earthly cage.

Short on breath and near the top,
he paused for a moment
to catch his breath.
It would be his last stop.

Looking around although beauty
did abound,
only darkness he felt.
Ignoring the sound of silence,
the peace of the path,
the peace of the day,
step by step he was on
top. No one was there.
No one to stop.

He took one look over the
cliff, down the ravine.
The highs and lows of mountains
jagged rocks, peaks, the valley
reminded him of his
failures and setbacks.

No, he would make one last
stop before leaping over the
edge.
He craved the water from
his pack.
He would pass on having
a snack.

The cool brisk water quenched his thirst.
It was time now.
He headed for the edge.

He began to leap without a sound.
In falling forward, he felt
a strong hand
land upon his shoulder.

A stranger's voice was heard
to say,
"You are loved
in so many ways."

The stranger pulled him back
to solid rock.
Then with a smile,
asked the young man if
he would sit
just a while.

"I guess," replied the young man.
Then the stranger suggested he
take off his pack
set it to the side.
Breathe, and rest a moment.
The stranger said,
"It is nice to have the weight of the world off your back."

"Yes," replied the young man
As the stranger smiled and
spoke, "Life, like that pack,
can become so full, so
heavy, so weighted down that
the burdens become too heavy
to carry, to move on."

The young man found himself
taken in with the peace of
the stranger's voice.
With what had led
to this day,
the young man's choice.

Next, the stranger asked the
young man if he knew that
each day brought change, each
day brought hope, each day
brought meaning, each day
brought opportunity, the chance
to begin
again?

The young man said that
his perspective had never
been of such great
hope as the stranger explained.

The young man then asked,
"Do you know that what you
have spoken is true?"
Peaceful words of the stranger
replied, "You are of infinite
worth, of value.
That is why I have chosen
to be here with you."

In quietness, the young man
sat with tear-filled eyes.
The reality of his decision,
he began to realize.

Then spoke the stranger in peace
and said, "Your greatest
gifts are yet to be found. You
have a long life yet to be
discovered. You will save others.
You will find love, you will
find much happiness, you will
leave a legacy. Your children
will help solve world hunger,
lead nations, and help bring
peace. Some will teach.
Some will be great mothers
and fathers.
What I have spoken
is only a small portion of

how you and your posterity
will make a difference, so never cease."

"We have spent time together
this beautiful day.
Might you share a little food
and water with me
if that's ok?"

The young man took out some
food, poured some water
in a cup.
Then shared it with a stranger.
As the stranger broke
bread, then
quenched his thirst
with the water from the
young man,
he did sup.

A few moments passed. The
stranger stood up then put
out his strong hand to the
young man and
motioned him to rise.
As the stranger took his
hand then pulled the
young man up,
he thanked the young man
for what they shared.

The young man, now on his
feet, pulled the stranger
close then gave him a
hug.

"So it's back down the
mountain," the stranger said.
"I believe you will go."

"Yes," said the young man.
"Thanks to you,
a new path
I do go."

As the young man turned to pick
up his backpack
from the ground,
the stranger
was nowhere
to be found.[23]

Perplexed but full of
life, a newfound hope,
a newfound vigor and joy,
down the mountain the young
man would bound.
Looking along the path he
found a walking stick.
As he reached and picked

Poems for Courage

it up,
he found the words were
etched,
"I was a stranger, and
Ye took me in."
The young man began to
wonder with whom
he had supped.

At the base of the mountain,
done with the trail,
he could not wait to
share the day.
The miracle
of such a
tale.

The wound prints in the
strangers'
hands and wrists
had changed this young
man's life.
He would
forever
insist.
His peaceful presence would
forever persist.

I find time to breathe, ponder, and reflect on

_____
_____
_____
_____
_____
_____
_____
_____
_____
_____
_____

*I find time for love, joy, and
take time to write about*

_____
_____
_____
_____
_____
_____
_____
_____
_____
_____
_____

*I take time to forgive and
release and write about*

_____
_____
_____
_____
_____
_____
_____
_____
_____
_____

*I take time to respect and prioritize
my endeavors and write about*

_____
_____
_____
_____
_____
_____
_____
_____
_____
_____

10
It Will Be All Right

A father loses his job.
The company closes, not by choice.
He then goes home,
only to hear his little son's voice.

"Daddy, how was your day?"
What does a father say?

"Oh son, being your dad
is my favorite job in the world."
Then with a hug, the father's hope
begins to renew.

That night as he looks
in the mirror,
reality reflects, it does appear.[24]

He tells his wife things
will be all right.
Then he opens his scriptures for
courage and insight.

That night it would be
easy to give up.
But he has a Higher Purpose,
a reason to get up!

He begins the day with
a prayer of gratitude.
Then with a smile, he
abounds with attitude.

O, the struggles he is aware.
But instead of fear he has
faith in what is to be.

A few weeks and months go
by. Then one day when he
walks in, his son smiles to say,
"Dad, it will be all right."[25]
The son smiles with the
greatest of faith.

A few days later the phone
rings. The call comes.
The offer is exactly what
was needed.
Could it be the faith of
the father or son?
Could it be the faith of
the family?

Or, blessings, prayers, and
miracles?
By love, it is done.

I find time to breathe, ponder, and reflect on

_____
_____
_____
_____
_____
_____
_____
_____
_____
_____
_____
_____

*I find time for love, joy, and
take time to write about*

_____
_____
_____
_____
_____
_____
_____
_____
_____
_____
_____
_____

*I take time to forgive and
release and write about*

_____
_____
_____
_____
_____
_____
_____
_____
_____
_____
_____

*I take time to respect and prioritize
my endeavors and write about*

_____
_____
_____
_____
_____
_____
_____
_____
_____
_____
_____

11
The Gift of Freedom

The price of freedom is very high.
Many have fought.
Many did die.[26]

May we never take for granted
the freedom we possess
for the price of
another's success.

Each day if you have this gift,
through some challenges
you may sift.

But take a few moments
and ponder through
the gift of freedom given
to you.[27]

A price far greater than
most could bear.
Make each minute count.
Show you care.

I find time to breathe, ponder, and reflect on

_____
_____
_____
_____
_____
_____
_____
_____
_____
_____
_____

*I find time for love, joy, and
take time to write about*

_____
_____
_____
_____
_____
_____
_____
_____
_____
_____

*I take time to forgive and
release and write about*

_____
_____
_____
_____
_____
_____
_____
_____
_____
_____
_____

*I take time to respect and prioritize
my endeavors and write about*

_____
_____
_____
_____
_____
_____
_____
_____
_____
_____
_____

12
In the Moment

I hear the water pouring over,
like words from the fall I
soon discover.

Golden rays touched my heart and soul.
What to the giver I owe.

Blue skies and cool crisp breeze.
What a moment to sit, I please.

Bubbling waves in the crested pool.
Not to notice, I'd be a fool.

Laughter is the best medicine, they say.
Along with the moment, a sunny day.

The bliss of life is the
moment I live.[28]
To give thanks to my maker
I must give![29]

I find time to breathe, ponder, and reflect on

_____
_____
_____
_____
_____
_____
_____
_____
_____
_____
_____
_____

*I find time for love, joy, and
take time to write about*

_____
_____
_____
_____
_____
_____
_____
_____
_____
_____
_____
_____

*I take time to forgive and
release and write about*

_____
_____
_____
_____
_____
_____
_____
_____
_____
_____

*I take time to respect and prioritize
my endeavors and write about*

_____
_____
_____
_____
_____
_____
_____
_____
_____
_____

13
On the Ropes

Upon exiting the locker room
and entering the dark hall,
the weathered boxing champion
could hear the roar of the crowd.
He could see the lights.
His family sitting front and center.
A last-minute check of his
clothing, then his gloves.
Once again stepping into the
lights, into the ring, doing what he loves.

Now, standing toe to toe
with a glare, a stare,
the referee let each boxer know
It was time to rumble – this would
be 12 rounds if each should go the
distance.

The champion was well-seasoned, well
trained. He knew losing. How to win,
how to get back up, how to handle pain.

The contender had worked hard, trained
hard. He would put it all on the
line, crawling up for this opportunity to fight.
He was a brawler.
His family by ringside, a wonderful sight.

A flurry of punches from the contender
inside and out.
Then a few body shots.
A left hook, a jab.
He was not holding back.
Nevertheless, the champion
could handle the attack.
His stance kept him rolling
with the punches. Might the
contender even have a chance?

Now into round three.
The contender had racked up the
score. Why was the champion
holding back? Was he too old or
out of shape? Was he done or
just having some fun?[30]

In the fourth round, the champion
let loose knocking the contender
to the mat for a seven count.
Shaken, bruised, a little bent, most
of his energy now spent.

Back on his feet clearly shaken,
looking at his wife, his
newborn son.
The win.
The purpose.
The prize almost taken.

With newfound strength the contender
did fight not knowing the
champion's insight to the contender's.
Like the surgery his son so desperately
needed. Yes, it was private but the
champion knew it was much more than
a fight.

With each round, the contender did
pound. With each round, the champion
did teach. Then in the eleventh, the
contender on the ropes heard the
champion say, "There's going to be
a miracle this day."

Toe to toe and pound for pound
around the ring they went until
the bell of the 12th did sound.
The champion knew soon into the
fight he could take the contender
or choose the right. He
had plenty to spare so tonight,

the winning purse to the contender
and his family to save his honor,
his son's sight. It's not always
about winning but sometimes instilling
courage and hope when we choose the right.[31]

I find time to breathe, ponder, and reflect on

_____
_____
_____
_____
_____
_____
_____
_____
_____
_____
_____
_____

*I find time for love, joy, and
take time to write about*

_____
_____
_____
_____
_____
_____
_____
_____
_____
_____
_____
_____

*I take time to forgive and
release and write about*

_____
_____
_____
_____
_____
_____
_____
_____
_____
_____

*I take time to respect and prioritize
my endeavors and write about*

_____
_____
_____
_____
_____
_____
_____
_____
_____
_____

14

Of the Heart

Some might have the
ongoing
bucket list full of
experiences or achievements
one hopes to accomplish
in this life.

While others adapt the
YOLO -
You Only Live Once
mindset, making decisions
in the moment.

Others have integrated both
bucket lists and YOLOs into
daily or weekly living.
Some with balance,
some very giving.[32]

What is really important
to you?
Remember, you are gifted.
There is only one of you.[33]

What will your legacy be?
What will you spiritually and temporally
experience and see?

On the journey we call
life.
This is a beautiful gift.

Take a moment, breathe in,
breathe out.
You are here, you have
purpose.
Your heart is beating.
You matter.
Therefore,
you have courage.

Keep going, the path will
not always be without
some challenges.
Know most of these will pass.
Turn the negative into a positive.

Your journey will have adventures.
You will accomplish much.
Remember what is truly important.
Remember to reflect on
all that is good,
all that you have overcome,
all that you have and
will do.

I find time to breathe, ponder, and reflect on

_____
_____
_____
_____
_____
_____
_____
_____
_____
_____
_____

*I find time for love, joy, and
take time to write about*

_____
_____
_____
_____
_____
_____
_____
_____
_____
_____
_____

*I take time to forgive and
release and write about*

_____
_____
_____
_____
_____
_____
_____
_____
_____
_____
_____

*I take time to respect and prioritize
my endeavors and write about*

_____
_____
_____
_____
_____
_____
_____
_____
_____
_____
_____
_____

15
True Friendship

A friend will be with you
through thick and thin.
A true friend
will endure even to the end.

A friend that is true,
has infinite value in more than
one way![34]
A true friend shares with you,
knowing what to say.

A friend may not see you
for quite a while.
But even if years pass,
you value their smile.

A friend may call you in
your time of need.
A friend may help you
to succeed.
A friend will love you at
the high.
A friend will love you at

the low.

A friend will be there
when many are not.
For a friend will know just
the right thought.

What kind of friend are you?
And as a friend,
what do you do?

What kind of friendship do
you share?
As a friend how do you
care?

What kind of friendship
have you shown?
For the kindness you share
kindness to be known.

A friend or friendship has
infinite worth.
A friend to the end that
started from birth.[35]

Perhaps a friendship that began
before here.
Eternal friend, I feel you
near.

I find time to breathe, ponder, and reflect on

_____
_____
_____
_____
_____
_____
_____
_____
_____
_____
_____

*I find time for love, joy, and
take time to write about*

_____
_____
_____
_____
_____
_____
_____
_____
_____
_____
_____

*I take time to forgive and
release and write about*

_____
_____
_____
_____
_____
_____
_____
_____
_____
_____

*I take time to respect and prioritize
my endeavors and write about*

_____
_____
_____
_____
_____
_____
_____
_____
_____
_____

16
Duty to Lift Up

We each have a duty to share.
To help the less fortunate.
To care.[36]

When someone is down and misfortune has arrived,
blessings to those who helped them survive.

There are so many with a lot.
There are so many with a little to be sought.

For it does not matter the quantity we give.
But what matters is we help each other to live.
Each are happy and measure does vary.
But given the chance another to carry.

Dreams and goals can be
far and wide.

We can lift one another or walk
beside.

There will be setbacks
and trials.
But to the prize as the
giver smiles.

Lifting the burdens and the
weight.
From another this surely
is the greatest of the great.

So if you are feeling
kind of low, ask
whom may you help?
What seeds to sow?
Lift another and feel the
spirit.
This is the voice of true
success.[37]

I hope you feel.
I pray you hear it.

What may come and what may go.
Truth has been spoken.
This I know.

I find time to breathe, ponder, and reflect on

_____
_____
_____
_____
_____
_____
_____
_____
_____
_____
_____
_____

*I find time for love, joy, and
take time to write about*

_____
_____
_____
_____
_____
_____
_____
_____
_____
_____
_____

*I take time to forgive and
release and write about*

_____
_____
_____
_____
_____
_____
_____
_____
_____
_____
_____

*I take time to respect and prioritize
my endeavors and write about*

_____
_____
_____
_____
_____
_____
_____
_____
_____
_____
_____
_____

17
Inner Strength

No matter how many times
you strike out,
get knocked down,
or knocked out.
No matter.

What matters is your perspective.
And how you deal with it.[38]
Get up.
Find the courage and
fortitude to go forward.

Everyone has setbacks or
will face defeat.
Stand up.
Get back.
Rise to your feet.

Do not let temporary defeat
win through cheat.
See beyond the setback.
See success.

"Be courageous; follow your heart?"
Get going, get moving.
Be about doing good.

So what if it takes a few
more strikes to have a home
run?
So what if dusting yourself off
and getting up
is how success is done?

Many great individuals have
faced failure or defeat.
That was not the end.[39]

History is filled with those
who have fallen
only to rise again.

Get up, get going, move forward.
Set your pace.
The prize goes to the runner who
finishes the race.

When a *warrior* of success
you have found,
Then lend your hand to another.
Help pick them up from being
knocked down.

I find time to breathe, ponder, and reflect on

_____
_____
_____
_____
_____
_____
_____
_____
_____
_____
_____
_____

*I find time for love, joy, and
take time to write about*

_____
_____
_____
_____
_____
_____
_____
_____
_____
_____
_____

*I take time to forgive and
release and write about*

*I take time to respect and prioritize
my endeavors and write about*

18
By My Side

What an incredible season
with an extraordinary team
vying for a world
championship title.

Sure, they lost a few games
but kept moving forward,
regrouped
and reflected.
Kept working
on the wins.[40]

Their defense players on
the field –
as the opponents released
the ball into the end zone,
only to have the ball tipped.

A seasoned coach of this
extraordinary team,
watching over his players
on the field,
on the sidelines.

Noticing his player kneeling
on one knee,
Coach could see
this young man's face
covered in tears.

All eyes watching
the tipped ball
as the defense knocked
it to the ground.
It shut the incredible opponents
down.

Roaring of players, coaches, and
crowds, flooded the field.
Time stopped for a moment
for the new world champions.

Coach intentionally looked at the
tear-filled face of his star
player, then asked, "Are you all right?"
"Yes," replied the player.
"A few years back my father passed,
I have not cried since. He was here, he had
his arms around me. He was by my side."

"I believe you," said the coach.
"I believe these things happen.
I believe in you.
I believe these kinds of spiritual
experiences will continue."[41]

I find time to breathe, ponder, and reflect on

_____
_____
_____
_____
_____
_____
_____
_____
_____
_____
_____
_____

*I find time for love, joy, and
take time to write about*

_____
_____
_____
_____
_____
_____
_____
_____
_____
_____
_____

*I take time to forgive and
release and write about*

_____
_____
_____
_____
_____
_____
_____
_____
_____
_____

*I take time to respect and prioritize
my endeavors and write about*

_____
_____
_____
_____
_____
_____
_____
_____
_____
_____

19
Take That First Step

What is holding you back
from your dreams?
What is the excuse?
What is the hurdle you use?

Recently, I listened to an
incredible soul
who set aside excuses
to follow his dreams.
To become a gifted musician.
Considering an injury
left him with no hands,[42]
this incredible soul
brings music to many.
To what do we owe
this miracle?
The dream he followed
he failed not.
And brings tears of
joy and inspiration
performing each show.

What is holding you back
from your dreams?
Miracles happen each day.
There is one greater
that can provide the way.

Consider the paraplegic who
was not content to sit.
He readjusted his perspective,
followed his heart and soul.
Twenty-six point two miles
later we give thanks a
new world record, an incredible
soul.

What is holding you back?
Even a bridled horse has
the chance to race I say.
Follow your dreams, follow your
heart.
Pick up, pick up the pace.

Consider the young woman
who lost both her legs.
This could bring down even
the most noble of souls.
But thanks and praise be
to her and her ways.
Many new world records
she does own.

What is holding you back
from your dreams from
following your heart?
Passion is the flame or
spark where it does start.

Hope is believing this
is a start.
Surround yourself in this
beauty, this art.

Consider the successful executives
with the Midas touch.
Then with change they find
themselves broke.

There is a difference between
broke and broken-hearted. They
did not lose their dream.
They did not lose their
heart.

Now instead of running a
big business,
they have their own
taking care of the poor
and needy.
So now who has found
success?
Were it not for adversity,

many would go hungry.
Their ability to adapt
brought blessings to many.

Letting go of fear,
a new perspective appears.
I believe they had help
from angels who were
near.[43]

What is holding you back
from your dreams?
You need to know.
Sometimes you must
let go, so you can
follow your passion,
follow your heart.

Consider the bridled horse
upon the track is where it
starts.
A chance to win.
Chance to pace.
No more excuses.
Follow your dreams.
Follow your passion.
Embrace your heart and soul.

I find time to breathe, ponder, and reflect on

_____
_____
_____
_____
_____
_____
_____
_____
_____
_____
_____

*I find time for love, joy, and
take time to write about*

_____
_____
_____
_____
_____
_____
_____
_____
_____
_____
_____

*I take time to forgive and
release and write about*

_____
_____
_____
_____
_____
_____
_____
_____
_____
_____

*I take time to respect and prioritize
my endeavors and write about*

_____
_____
_____
_____
_____
_____
_____
_____
_____
_____
_____

20
It Matters to Me

Sometimes it is very easy
to give.
Especially when it has no
real impact
on the way
we live.

But to give when you have
very meager?[44]
Many have hesitated
some are not so eager.

Here the challenges that I
would propose.
Look into your heart.
Do what the Creator
would do.
The one that gives you everything.
Your breath of life.
All that is good.
All that is great.
What to propose?

Yes, He knows.
But to give when you have a small amount?
It's not the size, trust me.
It all counts.[45]

I find time to breathe, ponder, and reflect on

_____
_____
_____
_____
_____
_____
_____
_____
_____
_____
_____

*I find time for love, joy, and
take time to write about*

_____
_____
_____
_____
_____
_____
_____
_____
_____
_____

*I take time to forgive and
release and write about*

_____
_____
_____
_____
_____
_____
_____
_____
_____
_____

*I take time to respect and prioritize
my endeavors and write about*

_____
_____
_____
_____
_____
_____
_____
_____
_____
_____

21
Rekindle Your Dreams

Have a discussion that
is possible
with a child.
They have not been conditioned
to think negatively.
Full of dreams,
passion so wild.

They speak of new inventions
or doctors to be.
Of the things to do
of all they see.

The many countries and places
to go.
Space travel and imagination.
This wise generation.[46]

Boundaries or limits very few
the same.
For up to us a value system
to instill.

Boundaries and limits they
don't fear.
Take a few moments to
listen,
to hear.

If years and setbacks or
a few challenges
you did face.
Take a few moments, look
back.
Look for your dreams.
Let not sadness
be the case.

Even the master speaks of
the little ones
which you once were.
They are dreamers, doers
greatness to be done.[47]

You can still achieve it.
You can still live it.
You may need some help.
You can dream it and see it
once more.
You can see it, I know
you can.
For greatness you were

meant.
It is part of a divine
plan.
I hope as a child, you understand.

I find time to breathe, ponder, and reflect on

_____
_____
_____
_____
_____
_____
_____
_____
_____
_____
_____

*I find time for love, joy, and
take time to write about*

_____
_____
_____
_____
_____
_____
_____
_____
_____
_____
_____

*I take time to forgive and
release and write about*

_____
_____
_____
_____
_____
_____
_____
_____
_____
_____

*I take time to respect and prioritize
my endeavors and write about*

_____
_____
_____
_____
_____
_____
_____
_____
_____
_____

22
Courage to Stand

Interesting how
things can work out,
when someone has
little doubt.

A discussion of Christians
was taking place.
Of believers and wonders
in this work space.

The time had extended
past the time of close.
Typically they'd be locking up
for the day ended.

Running late they walked outside
to see a vehicle hit the place
where they typically were.
Had they been there,
they would have been
seriously hurt.
From the report,

possibly died.[48]
They found themselves on
the way to help.[49]
Busted, bleeding they found
him there.
Probably not a site some
would bear.

As the evening unfolded, the
help did come.
With angels to some.

The one who had brought
this terrible impact
would take time to heal.
Would live, I knew this fact.

Believers and wonders both
did learn.
A newfound faith
all did earn.

The change it had for the
better that day.
It brought them all closer.
Each found their way.

I find time to breathe, ponder, and reflect on

_____
_____
_____
_____
_____
_____
_____
_____
_____
_____
_____
_____

*I find time for love, joy, and
take time to write about*

_____
_____
_____
_____
_____
_____
_____
_____
_____
_____
_____
_____

*I take time to forgive and
release and write about*

_____
_____
_____
_____
_____
_____
_____
_____
_____
_____

*I take time to respect and prioritize
my endeavors and write about*

_____
_____
_____
_____
_____
_____
_____
_____
_____
_____

23
We All Matter

Dreams may come and go.
They can come apart.
They can shatter.

We all matter to Him.[50]

You can lose and not be
lost.
Go upside down financially the cost.
Acquiring education and experience,
so all is not lost.

We all matter to Him.

Health setbacks other
challenges too.
Come what may.
Sometimes they do.

We all matter to Him.
Overwhelming challenges
many face.

Where are the answers?
Seek to know his grace.

We all matter to Him.

Choice allowed you take the
journey, your path.
He can mend the broken.
Turn away the wrath.

We all matter to Him.

When the darkened grey skies
come upon you,
remember:

We all matter to Him.

When blackness the thief of
hope comes by.
Let it pass.
Let it pass.
Like clouds in the sky.

We all matter to Him.
For the warmth of the
sun.
It will shine.[51]
We all matter to Him.

I find time to breathe, ponder, and reflect on

_____
_____
_____
_____
_____
_____
_____
_____
_____
_____
_____

*I find time for love, joy, and
take time to write about*

_____
_____
_____
_____
_____
_____
_____
_____
_____
_____
_____

*I take time to forgive and
release and write about*

---

*I take time to respect and prioritize
my endeavors and write about*

24
Here With Me

By two hands a life
was spared.[52]
The traffic was moving fast.
The vehicle at about seventy
went off the freeway
into the air.

Upon seeing this horrific
life-changing
event,
the vehicle had landed
in a ravine.
The metal crumpled.
Wrinkled, bent.

Passersby suddenly stopped
or pulled to the side.
Temporal angels ran over[53]
to help.
Faces of sadness, shock
disbelief, tears.

The young man was not
of many years.
Hunched over bleeding.
Sounds of sadness.
You could feel the tears.

Apparently, he was traveling
with friends
from a game.
They tried to open the
vehicle but bent and broken,
it was not the same.

Would this be the last time
they saw their friend?
Is this how this young
man's
life would end?

They tried with all their
might to get in.
Their friend hunched over.
No movement.
No breath.
Was this his death?
Then over the hill
into the embankment,
a young man came.
He picked up a large

boulder, and threw it through
the back side window.
It shattered in pieces.
Shattered the seal.

He reached in and unlocked
the door.
Opened it and
saw no breath
or life at all.

Turned to the friends with
another,
then asked may we offer
a prayer?
A blessing or more.

Without hesitation, his
friend said yes.
Shaken up and deeply
concerned.
Of unknown angels
they were about to learn.
The prayer was offered.
It was heaven-sent
Their friend sat up,
heaven's breath sent.
Is it not interesting? I find
that the young man who

took out the window
and stood in prayer
was a prodigal son
who was sent that day.

He did not know the driver
of the event.
But I feel it's safe to say
crossing paths were divinely
or Heaven-sent.

Never underestimate the
strength of Divine power.
For the call can come
at any hour.

Never underestimate what
you can do.
For either of them
could have been
me or you!

I find time to breathe, ponder, and reflect on

_____
_____
_____
_____
_____
_____
_____
_____
_____
_____
_____

*I find time for love, joy, and
take time to write about*

_____
_____
_____
_____
_____
_____
_____
_____
_____
_____
_____

*I take time to forgive and
release and write about*

_____
_____
_____
_____
_____
_____
_____
_____
_____
_____

*I take time to respect and prioritize
my endeavors and write about*

_____
_____
_____
_____
_____
_____
_____
_____
_____
_____

25
A Time to Rise Up

Many choose to live far below
their divine potential.
If they are happy,
their lives are fulfilled.
Then purpose they have found.[54]

But if sadness or a yearning
in your heart
cries out for change or
more,
then one must live.
Oh, yes, one must give.

You need to listen to your
heart and soul.
To your divine creator.
To both you owe.

Somewhere or someone or
something or some event
has allowed you to settle.
Yes, I admit.

There are times in each
of our lives we might
have to take a break.
Believe me though
you have a life's dream.
A life's work.

To settle below your potential.
To not follow your heart.
To not draw upon your divine
plan.
This is surely to not understand.
Is surely a mistake.

Settle no more.
Start moving in the direction
of your choice.
If you need help,
open your mouth.
You're right.
Let others
hear your voice.

Find individuals with common
dreams, goals, and values you share.
Live life to the fullest.
Live as if you care.

Create the life you would want
to live.
When it arrives to others
you must give.

You are here to help make
a change.
When your life has found
what you seek,
help others arrange.

If you think living below
your divine potential is
rough,
think about missing all of
your dreams.
Or seeing but a few.
See a full life.
Chart the new.

Could have, should have.
I have heard them all.
There are more.
There are vices.
They close the doors.
They bring the sorrow.
Yes, this one maybe tomorrow.

To your heart, your soul this
day.
Follow or find the divine greatness.
Your destiny;
live this way.[55]

I find time to breathe, ponder, and reflect on

_____
_____
_____
_____
_____
_____
_____
_____
_____
_____
_____
_____

*I find time for love, joy, and
take time to write about*

_____
_____
_____
_____
_____
_____
_____
_____
_____
_____
_____

*I take time to forgive and
release and write about*

_____
_____
_____
_____
_____
_____
_____
_____
_____
_____
_____

*I take time to respect and prioritize
my endeavors and write about*

_____
_____
_____
_____
_____
_____
_____
_____
_____
_____
_____
_____

26
Opportunity in Adversity

I have seen the pain.
Friends lose homes or jobs.
Other material things.
Pain is the song
their heart sings.

Fear sets in, they question
all that was.
All that happens.
Why me?[56]
Was it because?

Sometimes they avoid others.
They shut out their friends.
Depression
or shaken confidence
sets in.[57]

If you are one of these
souls,
my heart, a prayer to you
we owe.

If you are not, out of kindness,
reversals can come to pass.
Don't let this opportunity to help go, alas!

Help, help now!
Whatever way it will
not matter how.
Please go and do.
Please help them.
Help them now!

If you're the soul that has been spent,
it's all right.
Even if you're down to your last cent.

I say call upon the Angels.
Kneel in prayer.
O, the angels
are out there
should you dare.

Base your worth on who you
are to become from this.
Not what you have or what you miss.

Call upon your angels, here and there!
Be prepared to live a full life.
Goodbye, despair!

I find time to breathe, ponder, and reflect on

_____
_____
_____
_____
_____
_____
_____
_____
_____
_____
_____
_____

*I find time for love, joy, and
take time to write about*

_____
_____
_____
_____
_____
_____
_____
_____
_____
_____
_____

*I take time to forgive and
release and write about*

_____
_____
_____
_____
_____
_____
_____
_____
_____
_____

*I take time to respect and prioritize
my endeavors and write about*

_____
_____
_____
_____
_____
_____
_____
_____
_____
_____

27
Nurtured By Nature

Have you ever seen,
a wounded creation nourished
back to Health?

A dog, a bird, the broken wing.
With love and kindness
they now sing.[58]

Takes a little time.
A lot of trust.
But with love, encouragement, and
a little time,
healing takes place.[59]
Friendships found
from this divine creature
lifted from the ground.

Just as the heavenly creatures
to fall,
it happens to some.
I pray not to all.

They are out there. It could
be your call.
Find them, help them,
pray for them all.

I find time to breathe, ponder, and reflect on

_____
_____
_____
_____
_____
_____
_____
_____
_____
_____
_____

*I find time for love, joy, and
take time to write about*

_____
_____
_____
_____
_____
_____
_____
_____
_____
_____
_____

*I take time to forgive and
release and write about*

_____
_____
_____
_____
_____
_____
_____
_____
_____
_____
_____

*I take time to respect and prioritize
my endeavors and write about*

_____
_____
_____
_____
_____
_____
_____
_____
_____
_____
_____

28
More Valuable Than Gold

A story was told of a driver
who was on the way to sell his
most valuable piece of gold.

On his way there, he noticed
another alongside the road.
Without a thought,
through a prompting he said,
he picked up this stranger.
To brighten his day.
To lighten the load.[60]

A few miles later, he dropped
in front of the house.
Then drove to the freeway
to sell. He went
on his way.

However the stranger insisted
some money he take.
He replied, "I did not do it
for that.

Please, I forsake."
"No," replied the stranger.
"I insist, this is for you,
I must do."

A few miles down the
freeway,
the Samaritan noticed he
was almost out of gas.
Time would come, time
would pass.

As the driver pulled in to
fill the tank,
he realized the cash he had just
been given
was just enough to help
fill the tank.

Without it, he would not have
made it to where he had to go to
sell his gold. He had to feed his
family; they counted on him.

Arriving at the place to
sell his gold,
shimmering in the light.
Yes, a sacrifice.
It would now be sold.

He had vowed when he took
the stranger's cash to return it
the following day. "All right," said the
stranger. "If you say."

A family member put him up
for the night.
And the very next day,
he was on the freeway
with the stranger in sight.

Thoughts of food for his family
went.
A few dollars.
Heaven sent.

When he arrived outside
of the stranger's home.
He was nowhere
to be found.

So he shared the same with
the girl who answered the door.[61]
Did this stranger exist?
Or was he an angel helping the downtrodden?

The driver made it home that
night to share with his wife.
More than one Samaritan
had impacted all of their lives.

I find time to breathe, ponder, and reflect on

_____
_____
_____
_____
_____
_____
_____
_____
_____
_____
_____

*I find time for love, joy, and
take time to write about*

_____
_____
_____
_____
_____
_____
_____
_____
_____
_____
_____

*I take time to forgive and
release and write about*

_____
_____
_____
_____
_____
_____
_____
_____
_____
_____

*I take time to respect and prioritize
my endeavors and write about*

_____
_____
_____
_____
_____
_____
_____
_____
_____
_____

29
Those Who Believe

We have seen the brave or wounded
battle physical ailments.
Not once,
but twice.
Some even more.
They go into remission
to fulfill their
dream, their life's work.
Their mission.[62]

We believe in miracles.

We have seen the ravages
of the elements.
Wipe out entire citizens
or communities.
Only to bring help from
around the world
from the heavens
and more.

We believe in miracles.

We have seen those left in
the wars for dead.
Somehow, some way,
they bend a knee,
they bow their heads.

We believe in miracles.

We have seen the veteran's
wife.
Give service to her war-
torn spouse.
Some dedicated their life.

We believe in miracles.

We have seen in the children
who have survived the affiliations
of abuse, disease, unthinkable
things.
To rise from the ashes and
to do great things.
To live a life.
As noble
as queens and kings.
To live life to the fullest.
To make a difference
in this life.
To make a change for greatness.

To be accomplished
in all things.

We believe in miracles.

We have seen one spouse
lose another.
Even a child or two.
To see the strength come
to help.
From many a sister or
brother.

We believe in miracles.

We know of a teenager
who was out on the
edge of life.
To wake from a sound
sleep.
To pull another from
drowning.
To save another.
To save a life.
To see their own worth.
To realize
it was no mistake.
Why they were put on earth
to then believe in their
Divine birth.

We believe in miracles.

Those who were at death's
door given only a few days.
By a couple of doctors then
a few weeks.
Rally back for many years.
To make peace.
To mend a fence.
Sharing words, giving love.
A smile.
A kind word.
Each day a new gift.
To do what's needed
for others.
For others to see
some joy, some
tears.
They have been close to
crossing.
Close to the spirit.
Some of them
quickly share the message
of life.
You only have to hear it.
The peaceful silence
before the noise.

We believe in miracles.[63]

I find time to breathe, ponder, and reflect on

_____
_____
_____
_____
_____
_____
_____
_____
_____
_____
_____

*I find time for love, joy, and
take time to write about*

_____
_____
_____
_____
_____
_____
_____
_____
_____
_____
_____

*I take time to forgive and
release and write about*

_____
_____
_____
_____
_____
_____
_____
_____
_____
_____
_____

*I take time to respect and prioritize
my endeavors and write about*

_____
_____
_____
_____
_____
_____
_____
_____
_____
_____
_____

30
Your Truth

All that you do, and[64]
all that you have,
is only a finite part
of all that
you truly are.[65]

I find time to breathe, ponder, and reflect on

_____
_____
_____
_____
_____
_____
_____
_____
_____
_____
_____
_____

*I find time for love, joy, and
take time to write about*

_____
_____
_____
_____
_____
_____
_____
_____
_____
_____
_____

*I take time to forgive and
release and write about*

_____
_____
_____
_____
_____
_____
_____
_____
_____
_____

*I take time to respect and prioritize
my endeavors and write about*

_____
_____
_____
_____
_____
_____
_____
_____
_____
_____
_____

31
Angels' Landing

In the darkest of times
following a cascade of
economic upheavals,
a successful businessman
now found himself on the
brink of despair.

Reaching for his phone,
he felt impressed to
call two close friends,
asking each if they had
time to meet.

Each agreed, heavy hearted.
He let his friends know
they would be looking at
some real estate. To wear
hiking shoes, and bring two water
canisters.

His phone conversation now
coming to an end,

he closed by saying he
was looking forward to meeting
up with both friends.
"You might enjoy the journey,
sights, and fresh air."

Arriving at the trail head
of the West Rim Trail,
a few smiles
a few hugs.
It's only a few miles
their friend, a businessman
was heard to say,
"This is the way."

Now summiting the trail
somewhat incredibly colorful
orange, crimson, reds,
some golds, some whites.

A few hours into the hike
the trail began to narrow
somewhat tight.

The higher they climbed
a noticeable peace,
a noticeable silence.
Each could hear the others'
steps.

Truly a place where songbirds
sing,
condors and eagles spread their
wings.

All were focused on the
narrowing trail with death-
defying, steep drop-offs.
A chain pulled through the
eye hook stakes that had
been driven into Jurassic-
age Navajo stone.

"We're almost there,"
spoke their friend
and businessman.
All the while, each pacing
themselves taking time to
breath in the fresh,
clean air.

Feeling the warmth of the
open sky, sun,
with their destination in sight,
the three took a moment
then a three-hundred sixty
degree view of this
open canyon.
Breathtaking –

Monolithic, all colorful.
A heavenly sight.

With a pleasant breeze
the sun shining upon them,
panoramic views of these
giant formations –
a majestic art,
truly a masterpiece.

Groves of various colored trees
on the canyon floors,
emerald green trees upon
some of the canyon walls.

Yes, this was Zion's National Park.
Home of the
Ancient Anasazi Cliff and
Stone Dwelling people.

With feet firmly on the
top of
Angels' Landing,[66] the three
looked at the few hikers,
some headed back down,
another sitting in silence.
possibly meditating or giving
thanks.
Then, in a small passage of

time, it was just the
three as if meant to be.

In a soft but positive
voice, one of the two
friends was heard to say,
"What's on your mind this day?"

Their friend and businessman
with tears in his eyes
replied, "I invited you both
to share with each of you,
I am going through a lot
of adversity. Would you be
willing to share a blessing
or prayer with me?" They
could see the pain and
humility in his eyes.

So it was given on top
of Angels' Landing that day.

Angels' Landing previously known
as Temple of Aeolus.

I would have to believe there
is great power and strength
in prayers, blessings, and temples.[67]

Each of the three have faced challenges and adversity.
They would be the first to share blessings, miracles, and prosperity.[68]

I find time to breathe, ponder, and reflect on

_____
_____
_____
_____
_____
_____
_____
_____
_____
_____

*I find time for love, joy, and
take time to write about*

_____
_____
_____
_____
_____
_____
_____
_____
_____
_____

*I take time to forgive and
release and write about*

_____
_____
_____
_____
_____
_____
_____
_____
_____
_____
_____

*I take time to respect and prioritize
my endeavors and write about*

_____
_____
_____
_____
_____
_____
_____
_____
_____
_____
_____

32
Breaking the Chains[69]

Praise to the father that
became a better father than
he had.
The abuse is gone, now he
spends his time
working with those children
who lost their way.
Many he took into his home
for on the streets
they had roamed.

He fed them and clothed
them.
Helped them through school.
This was his passion.
Making a difference
he had to do.
Most are grown now with
families of their own.
Where would they be without his
love?
For this is what he came to do.

He made the world a better
place for you.

He walked away from
success by the world's measure.
to help, to serve, to be better.

He followed his dreams.[70]
He followed his heart.
Giving each child a new start.[71]

I find time to breathe, ponder, and reflect on

_____
_____
_____
_____
_____
_____
_____
_____
_____
_____
_____

*I find time for love, joy, and
take time to write about*

_____
_____
_____
_____
_____
_____
_____
_____
_____
_____
_____

*I take time to forgive and
release and write about*

_____
_____
_____
_____
_____
_____
_____
_____
_____
_____

*I take time to respect and prioritize
my endeavors and write about*

_____
_____
_____
_____
_____
_____
_____
_____
_____
_____

33
Blue Coast Courage

With his feet now upon the
warm golden sand,
his board by his side,
firmly in hand.

A moment to look out over
the vast aqua blue, deep
emerald green ocean. The
sound of the crashing salty
waves only seemed to
call his name.
A life goal, a dream.
If asked, he would say,
"Do the things you love
as I will each day."

Out into the sea a
smile upon his face.
How far you say
to ride the North Shore
waves.
A place of many

pro championships.
It was about his journey,
Pipeline an incredible place.

Breathtaking, where Aumakua spirits
and wave-riders find grace.
His heart pounded not out
of fear.
He was about to catch
an incredible wave.
Time for
take off
was near.

Living the best life was
part of his plan.
Living to the fullest potential.
Facing what some might
consider
their greatest
fear.[72]

Doing now, something he loved.
A young boarder chasing
his dreams.
Not wasting time
with inanimate
things.
Living the best of life to

follow his heart.
Listening to his spirit.
The roar of the ocean sings.

Dropping in then down the
straight, the energy of
the ocean wave
sent this young boarder
on an amazing
ride. You should see his
board glide
across the
ocean water.
Making the day
great.

As waves began to slow,
back out into the aqua
blue emerald green water
he would go.
Living his best life.
All the while,
nourishing his soul.

When, without warning,
and some might fear,
a bomber of a fast heavy
wave would descend upon
him. The power of the ocean

breaking his board in two.
Into the dark depth below
the wave riding boarder would go.

Many early dawn patrol
hours on the surf and
board team he had trained.
Practicing, playing in the
warmth of the sun.
The cool of the rain.

Now the force of the waves,
the weight of the water
had the advantage.
If he lost his faith
or began to panic,
this could be the end.

All the while, holding his breath
a moment of the beauty
the ocean floor offered
to share.
He knew with his
respect of the
ocean,
the beauty of the living
creatures there.
His creation, he knew he
would have limited time

to spare.
Before using all of his oxygen,
then gasping for air.

No he would not die today.
He chose life.
He chose not to panic.[73]
But have peace in his
heart.
He would focus,
conserve his oxygen.
Let the current
of the water and waves
recede.
The prayer of that early
morning prior to entering
the water he would now
need.

Now it was time. He had
gone deeper than he wanted
to be.
Some time had passed.
Possibly two
or three minutes.
Maybe more.
With all of his courage,
all of his strength.
Back to the top

off the ocean floor.
He could see the sunlight
just a little further.
A little more.

He had pulled his back out of
the sea cave
reef.
Now breaking through
the salty
ocean surface,
he took a deep
breath filling his
lungs with precious
coastal air and
oxygen.

Only to find himself wrapped
up in a barreling wave.
Once again to be pushed well
below the surface.
The force and weight of
the ocean once again had
the upper hand.
He would not panic.
He chose to conserve his
energy
and oxygen to use wisdom.
He knew fighting against

the strength and weight of
the ocean was useless.
Let it once again pull back,
recede.

Remain and he continued to
think, to remain calm. These
were the words flowing through
his mind.
Today is a great day to live.
As the ocean
began to recede,
this time drawing upon
courage and
strength beyond
his own.
This sixteen-year-old
boarder once again
broke through
the salty ocean
surface.
This time,
gasping for air, but he
had made it.
No he would not die
today.
Pipeline was for victors
and champions.
A sacred place.

This young boarder
would say.

Finding the safest route
into the beach shoreline
was now the
task.
God puts the right people
in our lives
if we but ask.
So this young humble
boarder
who had a love of the
sea.
A love of creatures,
of God's magnificent
creations.

Turned upon hearing a voice
calling out,
"Are you all right?"
"Yes," replied the boarder
over the sound of
waves.
The professional photographer
asked the boarder, "Would
you like to follow me
back to shore?
I have been here many

years before, follow me."

An answer to the young
boarder's heart.
Now swimming through
a few rough currents,
a few waves.
The aqua blue and emerald
green coastal
water.
The young boarder had learned
the gifts of
how to survive.
How to thrive.
How to remain calm.
How to be at peace.
The blessings of timing.
The gifts of courage and strength.
The blessings of the morning sun.

His heart full of gratitude.
His guide back to the
shore, he
did thank
with his feet.
Now upon the
warm sand,
no board in
hand,

he did stand.

Upon the shore line, he now
did walk.
Greetings and words of deep
concern.
From his sister,
his mother, and father.
Many others,
then a few hugs.
And expressions of love.

As the young boarder now
sat on the beach in
the warm sand next
to family, next to his
Dad.
There was the sound of
the roaring twenty-five
foot waves and the
warmth of the sun, the
sprays of the salty ocean,
the silence of the young
boarder who had accomplished
his goal and fulfilled a dream.

Yes, it was a good day to be alive.

Then, after a few minutes

and what seemed like a
calm in the waves,
the young boarder turned
to his father and said,

"Dad, you know last year
when my heart stopped?"
"Yes, son."
"And I came back."
"Yes, son."
"I knew I
would be all right. I just
had to be calm, listen,
get a feel for the current,
and I would make it out."
The dad replied, "I am so
Grateful you made it out.
You know you're loved, right?"
The dad replied.
"Yes," said
The son. Each had tear-
filled eyes. Then the son
replied, "You know, Dad, pipe
changed me."
"In what way?"
the dad responded.
"For the better,"
the son responded.
"How's that?"

"I had time to really think
about life."
The dad asked,
"Was it a spiritual experience?"
"Yes," responded the son. "Yes it was."

There was silence after
that. Only the roaring
of the incredibly large
waves that shimmered their
aqua blue
emerald green beauty
as if to say
"This is our day."

You should know this young
boarder, a respecter
of creatures and nature.
Dropped from sudden cardiac
arrest when he was only
fifteen.
Many people of all walks
of faith fasted and prayed
for him.
He was given CPR for twelve
minutes the first time, but
they would lose him twice
more. He spent many hours
in the ER and a few days

in critical care. A walking
miracle today. He would share
that God lives. His son lives
and, "Today is a great day
to be alive so make each day count."

I find time to breathe, ponder, and reflect on

_____
_____
_____
_____
_____
_____
_____
_____
_____
_____
_____
_____

*I find time for love, joy, and
take time to write about*

_____
_____
_____
_____
_____
_____
_____
_____
_____
_____
_____
_____

*I take time to forgive and
release and write about*

---

*I take time to respect and prioritize
my endeavors and write about*

34
The Path of Giants

There are many wise
souls, who walk this
land.
So eager to help,
to mentor,
to lend
a hand.

Choose, not to struggle
on this pathway alone.[74]

Strength these giants have,
they do possess.
Some very humble.
Some not.
But so full of wisdom.
It came with challenges.
It came at a price.
Having walked the
path before us,
they have already
sought.

By your voice, the courage
you must find.
Giants to seek
the real goldmine.
If you find the right
ones for you,
they can help,
they can mentor.[75]
Possibly a shorter path to
success.
I hope for you.

Their wisdom came over
the years.
Some will hear.
Some will not.
What you have found?
A teacher sought.

Success is yours, a gift
to share.
I have learned much,
this I can say.
From giants,
mentors, can be
some of the greatest
teachers.
Find those in common.
The path I say.
Learn of their wisdom;
a prosperous way.

I find time to breathe, ponder, and reflect on

_____
_____
_____
_____
_____
_____
_____
_____
_____
_____
_____
_____

*I find time for love, joy, and
take time to write about*

_____
_____
_____
_____
_____
_____
_____
_____
_____
_____
_____
_____

*I take time to forgive and
release and write about*

_____
_____
_____
_____
_____
_____
_____
_____
_____
_____

*I take time to respect and prioritize
my endeavors and write about*

_____
_____
_____
_____
_____
_____
_____
_____
_____
_____

35
You Have Purpose[76]

A lot of times greatness
grows from necessity.
The world is full of items
or things
you may not know the
inventor or the story
behind the breakthroughs and
inventions.
We have seen and
used a great read.
Search some of them
out.
You might find your muse.

A young mother set out
to raise a family
like future mothers
hope to do.

In the process of the
growth,
she was gifted with

a very special soul.
For this gift a change
would be made.
A way when there
was not one.
She had a dream of foresight.

Her daughter would be the
force.
A legacy that would roll
across many nations.
It would allow other
special souls to develop.
To share.
To bring the hearts of
special few to the many.
Medals would shine.
Accomplishments made.
No one would
be left behind.
She, the mother was lifted
by this gifted soul.
To leave a legacy of
greatness.[77]
For many know
because of both their
hearts, their dreams.
While there is more to the
story than I can say.

May all find such a way.
At this time, over three
million athletes in one hundred
fifty countries do compete.
From these special souls, we
see there is a way.

I find time to breathe, ponder, and reflect on

_____
_____
_____
_____
_____
_____
_____
_____
_____
_____
_____

*I find time for love, joy, and
take time to write about*

_____
_____
_____
_____
_____
_____
_____
_____
_____
_____
_____

*I take time to forgive and
release and write about*

_____
_____
_____
_____
_____
_____
_____
_____
_____
_____

*I take time to respect and prioritize
my endeavors and write about*

_____
_____
_____
_____
_____
_____
_____
_____
_____
_____
_____

36
Inspirational Drive

Talk about not letting
things stand in your way.
A few days ago, a son
walked into his father's
office. He was busy. It was a
typical stressful day.

His son asked, "Dad, have
you ever seen extreme
wheelchair?"[78]
"No," replied the father,
and went back to
work.

A few days later, the
father, although still in
the work mind,
took a few minutes and
searched out what
his son had asked
him to find.

The father sat quietly
as the video clip
began to play.
He saw the wheelchairs
moving all around.

A few minutes more he
watched one do a complete
flip and go upside down.
Airborne.
Into flight.
Off the ground.
Then he saw the young
man smile.
An indescribable sight
to see.

The father sat for a moment
and realized
that his young
son,
had put everything into
perspective.

Sometimes, we have to let
go.
We have to have faith
in the infinite creator.
We have to not hold
back.

Live to smile, like the
young man in the air.
His son knew he had to share.

Recently, I spoke to a
friend
whom I had not seen for
a while.

A few years back he was
training for a marathon.
Then,
without warning,
he was taken ill.

He became very sick he
could barely
get around.

He shared with me,
a sleepless night,
here he lay awake,
while his whole body
did ache.

He said he thought of how
he would not be able to
care for his children,
his spouse.

He began to pray. He even
asked to come home
to leave his earthly body.

A few months before this
night of prayer,
to test,
another friend of his
already had a
brush with death.

Now home to rebuild his
health,
his life.
A product had appeared.
A nutritional and medical path
for him and his wife.

A mutual friend who loved
them both
was moved to
open his mouth.

Upon learning of the stress and pain
in the middle of the storm,
in the middle of the rain.
The physical and spiritual pain,
he could not rest.

The door would open.
He replied, "You need to start.
I share this with you.
As you know,
I almost left.
It was my heart.

"I have learned a lot since then.
I felt impressed to come and share with you,
what I have been doing.
I use the best of science and the best of nutrition combined with prayer and exercise. I am here for you."

Here is value of divine guidance.
For him, he opened the door.
The one who delivered it followed
his heart.
The one who spoke to them
only sent love to them.

There is a little more
to the tale.
Recently, my friend
completed the marathon.
He said he had not
been sick in seven years.
Have I got your attention?
Please do hear.

He spends a good portion
of his life now
showing others,
teaching them how.

Not bad for a guy who was
on the highest pain meds
he could take.
Who wanted to leave so
his family he
would not forsake.

When there is a higher
will,
with divinity's help,
the heart in hand
but will be accomplished.
Health or ill
can we accept His will?[79]

I find time to breathe, ponder, and reflect on

_____
_____
_____
_____
_____
_____
_____
_____
_____
_____
_____

*I find time for love, joy, and
take time to write about*

_____
_____
_____
_____
_____
_____
_____
_____
_____
_____
_____

*I take time to forgive and
release and write about*

_____
_____
_____
_____
_____
_____
_____
_____
_____
_____

*I take time to respect and prioritize
my endeavors and write about*

_____
_____
_____
_____
_____
_____
_____
_____
_____
_____

37
Beyond the Hunger[80]

The oldest of four, he
had lost his father.
While looking after his
brothers, his sister,
his mother was
stricken.[81]

He recalls although it was
a dark time,
there were miracles.

One afternoon it came to
his attention.
As the fridge,
the cupboards
had all been
gone through.
They were empty.
No food or groceries.
The cupboards bare.
As the eyes of his sister,
his brother
peered upon him,

he felt the weight of
their tears.

He went back through the
cupboards.
Tried to wake his
Mother.
Not feeling well, asleep
she would be.

One more look into the
fridge. A little water
under the sink.
A little cleaner.

He looked back at the
eyes
who helped him know.
A time for action.
A time to rise.

He took one of his brothers,
climbed on a trike.
They headed down the sidewalk.
What a sight.

You could not tell those
two they were broke or
poor.

They had set out on a
mission.
You could not tell them
it could not happen.
For they had already gone
into action.
They were raggedy and worn,
hungry and torn.
What a sight.

A few blocks later, they found
a trash dumpster. It was too
big for either to climb in.
But this would not stop them.
The oldest brother was able
to lift the younger
brother up so he could climb
to the top.
Out came the goods. The little
brother did not stop.
Blues, greens, reds, yellows
now lay upon the ground.
What had these two found?

Loaded up on the trike,
they headed back to the
start.
To them, their find was worth
more than great art.

They took the cleaner they
had found.
Scrubbed each find with the
water hose
upon the ground.
As they finished their work,
they from the
hose did drink.
For it filled the belly.
The growls did shrink.

Then back on the trike
they did go.
Offering to strangers
their finds
to show.

First a few cents here
and there.
Then a few dollars
to help the way.
Then along came an angel.
They heard him say,
"How much for all
if I buy today?"
The angel took all that
was left. A smile to give.
There would be food to live.

As the two young brothers

returned from the street,
Mother and sister and
all could eat.

The stares now turned
to smiles.
He remembers it today.

Now, much older,
it appears
when there's no hope in
sight. When he faces challenges
of the day,
it's the hunger that gave him
courage and strength
he would say.

He reflects back upon this time.
Feels he is blessed
as we each are.
He has been blessed. He
believes.
We come here for success.
Angels are close.
Sometimes far.
He knows they're real.
He knows that
nothing is impossible. We are
born from divinity,
You are.

I find time to breathe, ponder, and reflect on

_____
_____
_____
_____
_____
_____
_____
_____
_____
_____
_____
_____

*I find time for love, joy, and
take time to write about*

_____
_____
_____
_____
_____
_____
_____
_____
_____
_____
_____
_____

*I take time to forgive and
release and write about*

_____
_____
_____
_____
_____
_____
_____
_____
_____
_____

*I take time to respect and prioritize
my endeavors and write about*

_____
_____
_____
_____
_____
_____
_____
_____
_____
_____

38
In Honor Of

Friends travel as we all
do.
Many different paths.
Some we stay in contact with.
Some we lose.
Some we hear from every
once in a while.

I had lost touch with one
who set out to achieve
many different
dreams and goals.

We met as kids when[82]
another
tried to get us both in
a fight
with each other.

Over the years, we both
set out on separate paths.
In order to

accomplish our goals,
we went our ways
over the years
with time.
We lost contact
as the world goes.

Then after almost 30 years,
a mutual friend
put us both in contact again.
I knew he was
a fighter, he had traveled the
world.

We visited a while. He told
me he had achieved every
thing he set out for.
Everything the world had
to offer.
Even more.

His motivation was real.
Very surreal.
He had won awards, been
recognized
by state.
Eaten at the finest places
while being part of
million-dollar deals.

He was now living with
a few animals.
A ranch in a small town.
Over the years,
he had been around.

While he continued to
share, feelings of
great emotion filled
the air.

With an earnest look
upon his face,
there was something
special about his pace.

Silence filled the air. I saw
tears flow into his eyes.
My friend who had been
most places,
worked most of his
years,
paused for a moment.
The words,
now tears.
I could feel that what
ever he was about to
say,
would have an impact.

For greatness.
For both of us that day.

"You know, my brother died
just before graduation.
He was only seventeen.
His heart gave out."

"Yes," I said.

He then let me know he
had done a lot
for him, his brother
who could not.

I felt from his words he
had achieved
on behalf of his brother first. On
his own behalf last.[83]

Looking back over the years,
I felt he could not
replace the loss.
For him, the greatest motivator
the price a cost.

I shared with him my
appreciation that he took time
to share.

The love for his brother,
his accomplishments,
his care.
Make time to help one
another.
Take time to share.

I find time to breathe, ponder, and reflect on

_____
_____
_____
_____
_____
_____
_____
_____
_____
_____
_____
_____

*I find time for love, joy, and
take time to write about*

_____
_____
_____
_____
_____
_____
_____
_____
_____
_____
_____

*I take time to forgive and
release and write about*

_____
_____
_____
_____
_____
_____
_____
_____
_____
_____

*I take time to respect and prioritize
my endeavors and write about*

_____
_____
_____
_____
_____
_____
_____
_____
_____
_____

39
Forty-five Cents

"Forty-five cents," he told me.
"I crossed the sea
to the country of opportunity."
I could see as he sat
across from me, he had
a few years on him
now.

His wall was covered with
pictures of those
famous.
Those who were
dignitaries.
Those who had touched
his life in one way
or another.

He pointed to a black and
white photo of a young man.
Very clean, a bit nostalgic.
Yes, a piece of history.

He shared his memory of
this now passed spirit.
The love and respect he
had for him, a spiritual
leader
for I did hear it.

All set aside some of
the poetic rhymes.
Focus back upon the
times.

He shared with me how he worked
and traveled some of the
world.
Opportunities came.
Yes, he met good fortune
crossed paths
with those of fame.

From forty-five cents to a
small fortune.
Two sons,
a wife who has
passed on.

He was working on putting
things in order.
Selling off a few holdings,

swimming each day.

The more we spoke, the
more I learned.
For success he no
longer strived.[84]

But from the fruits of his
labors,
happiness derived.

From forty-five cents to a
millionaire.
A gentleman too.
Would you dare?

From forty-five cents to
high end collectable.
A lot more.

We visited one of his sons. He
said we would meet.
Showed me his Rolls
Royces.
An *Incredible* feat.

He was true to his words.
A phone call, introduction
to both.

Then lunch to follow.
We shared some food,
some laughs,
some stories of their
Father.

Shortly after we met, their
Father passed away.
I will never forget his
humble beginnings.
The kindness he shared.
The stories, the dignitaries
or the
Rolls Royces.

I find it interesting still
that from forty-five cents he
did rise.[85]
He never spoke of poverty
or said "poor me."
But spoke of family,
friends, where he had been.
Those he remembered,
what he had seen.
I had the feeling I had

met a dignitary too.
How forty-five cents he
remembered through

the years.

I believe it motivated
him.
Kept him on the go.
I think he focused on
what could be.
Paid little attention to what
could not.

What could you or I turn
forty-five cents into?
Or would we focus on its
limited amount?

There are many places you
can feed an entire family
for forty-five cents.

What can you do with what
you have?
Only time will tell.
Use it well.

I find time to breathe, ponder, and reflect on

_____
_____
_____
_____
_____
_____
_____
_____
_____
_____
_____
_____

*I find time for love, joy, and
take time to write about*

_____
_____
_____
_____
_____
_____
_____
_____
_____
_____
_____
_____

*I take time to forgive and
release and write about*

_____
_____
_____
_____
_____
_____
_____
_____
_____
_____

*I take time to respect and prioritize
my endeavors and write about*

_____
_____
_____
_____
_____
_____
_____
_____
_____
_____

40
Why Not You?

Recently a study was
reported to reflect
that somewhere
between 15 to 20 percent
of all million-dollar
businesses
were started with less
than $5,000 dollars.[86]

So would this not be
another reflection.
How by small and
simple means,
great things
can come to pass.

Is it any different than
when a young child
on a hot day
decides to
take to the market
lemonade?

Yet I hear adults; some
complain
only if it was not so
hot.

What happens between
childhood
to adulthood?

Let's not lose our
perspectives.
Or sell out our dreams
or ourselves.

Sure, I have heard it
said that
sometimes
we have to live
in the meantime.

I see no problems with
the meantime.
As long as it
is not every time.

Five thousand to a million.
Why not?
Develop the perspective
of the child[87]

with lemonade
on a sunny day.
Heat was the opportunity.
Lemonade the product.
All things are possible!
Why not?

I find time to breathe, ponder, and reflect on

_____
_____
_____
_____
_____
_____
_____
_____
_____
_____
_____

*I find time for love, joy, and
take time to write about*

_____
_____
_____
_____
_____
_____
_____
_____
_____
_____
_____

*I take time to forgive and
release and write about*

_____
_____
_____
_____
_____
_____
_____
_____
_____
_____

*I take time to respect and prioritize
my endeavors and write about*

_____
_____
_____
_____
_____
_____
_____
_____
_____
_____
_____

41
In the Service of Others

Born in 1923 to a family
of ten,
his journey here
before the great depression
would begin.

At seven years old, he began
to get up at five AM.
The paper route
helped put food on the table
for his brothers, sisters,
and mother.

His father fell sick and
was called home
shortly after
his arrival here.

Never afraid to go out,
take care of what
was needed.
He made sure his

family never
went hungry.
Even if he went
with little
or without.

He knew hunger.
He knew hungry.
There is a difference
but both need food.[88]

When he got older, he acquired
his first automobile.
Then out of love
of country
and freedom,
he served in the military.

While he was serving
his family,
his mother
fell upon hard times
again.
Once again,
he helped.
He sacrificed.
His automobile was sold.
He continued to help.

The years went by as
some of his family too.

Later, he secured a job
that would allow him to
make a decent earning.
All the time,
grateful.
Yes, learning.

He was a gifted businessman.
Ideas, inventions
flowed
through his mind.

He was promised a promotion.
Vice-president
was discussed.
Still learning.

His invention was taken. The
vice-president position
filled by another.

This would take the wind
out of many a man.
But this defeat
was only the beginning
of greatness to come.
It was not the end.

He left that company and moved
to another state.
He started his own company,
first rate.

Modified his genius, then
never looked back.
Opened new markets,
sculpting a life.

Business success would follow.
Destiny met.
Was it a gamble?
A calculated risk?[89]
I bet.

His family grew. So did his
wealth.
Both have great value
as your health.

Millions came, his wealth
had grown.
From the cup of sweet
success
he did drink.
From poverty, the brink
the cup of success to drink.

I find time to breathe, ponder, and reflect on

_____
_____
_____
_____
_____
_____
_____
_____
_____
_____
_____

*I find time for love, joy, and
take time to write about*

_____
_____
_____
_____
_____
_____
_____
_____
_____
_____
_____

*I take time to forgive and
release and write about*

_____
_____
_____
_____
_____
_____
_____
_____
_____
_____

*I take time to respect and prioritize
my endeavors and write about*

_____
_____
_____
_____
_____
_____
_____
_____
_____
_____

42
A Mother's Love

Take the mother who
never quit.
She never gave up.[90]

Her daughter up to the
age of four was
seldom sick.
Then, one morning,
she was found lifeless
upon the floor.

She never gave up.

Seven years of medical
expertise.
Three near death
experiences.

She never gave up.

One day in the market,
her daughter asked

"Would I still be sick
in heaven?"
After a long pause,
tear-filled eyes,
her mother looked to her child
then replied, "No, my daughter."
To which she replied, "I
think I would like to go
to heaven then."

She never gave up.

Fasting came from family
to friends.
Her mother
determined
this would not be the
end.
She knew that people would
come.
Some would go.
But she felt in her heart
this was
not the end.

She never gave up.
After the fast, an angel
found.
She had already seen the
best for care.

Was this for real? Should
she raise her hopes?
Should the cure
be there?

This lifeless child began
to heal.
Faith of this mother, her
strength, surreal.

Months passed, miracles to
the quest for life.
A child to dream.

The darkness passed.
The story goes.
She achieves her
dreams and her milestones.
Accepted into many schools.
And was given one of the greatest
gifts of all:
motherhood.
This peaceful spirit
enjoys each day.

So do miracles happen even
now today.
Ask her mother,
who never gave up.[91]

I find time to breathe, ponder, and reflect on

_____
_____
_____
_____
_____
_____
_____
_____
_____
_____
_____
_____

*I find time for love, joy, and
take time to write about*

_____
_____
_____
_____
_____
_____
_____
_____
_____
_____
_____
_____

*I take time to forgive and
release and write about*

_____
_____
_____
_____
_____
_____
_____
_____
_____
_____
_____

*I take time to respect and prioritize
my endeavors and write about*

_____
_____
_____
_____
_____
_____
_____
_____
_____
_____
_____

43
Your Mind

Teachers. We should never
underestimate
the infinite
value of a
great teacher.[92]

A few years ago with as
little as five-hundred
dollars,
and a new perspective in
Biology,
a teacher took action
and believed.

The five-hundred was
turned into
fifty-thousand
in a short amount
of time.
You see, he believed in
what he had.
So much he was not

afraid to share.
And share he did.

One of his first clients
inquired.
"Why, why was the price
higher
than all the rest?"
"Simple," he replied.
"No one else
has this remarkable
breakthrough.

"I will stand behind my
product.
Behind my word."
The deal was
done.

After the client learned
more about the breakthrough,
a friendship was earned.

Now instead of five-hundred
dollars, this young teacher now
had
fifty-thousand.
With a commitment for
another four-hundred and

fifty-thousand.

That one client, that
one idea
now bore fruit of
five-hundred-thousand or
half a million plus.
The job, he finished.

It does not end there. Over
the course of a few more
years,
this little five-hundred
grew to
fourteen million plus.

So it is that the value of
this teacher,
I say was not
only
one of the successes.

Teachers plant many seeds.
Although this was only
one of the harvest.
How many would his
students pick from?
How many seeds would
keep giving?

The value of a great idea
combined with the value of
a great client
brought together
with action.

Resulted in wealth, yes,
but success too.

Because of great teachers,[93]
we can accomplish
our dreams.
If we but
follow through.

The majority of successful
people I have
met or learned from,

were taught or mentored
by great teachers.
They can be, I submit
one and the
same.

I find time to breathe, ponder, and reflect on

_____
_____
_____
_____
_____
_____
_____
_____
_____
_____
_____
_____

*I find time for love, joy, and
take time to write about*

_____
_____
_____
_____
_____
_____
_____
_____
_____
_____
_____
_____

*I take time to forgive and
release and write about*

_____
_____
_____
_____
_____
_____
_____
_____
_____
_____
_____

*I take time to respect and prioritize
my endeavors and write about*

_____
_____
_____
_____
_____
_____
_____
_____
_____
_____
_____

44
From the Ashes

Shortly after completing the
dream,
many years of planning, and time,
the beautiful lodge
nestled deep in the
pines of Montana
emerged.[94]

Standing on the deck or
glancing out the windows,
you could see the lakes,
golden eagles,
emerald forest trees,
even the painter of light
would be pleased.

Crisp sweet pines radiated
through the air.
Breezes from the snowcapped
cool mountains
permeated to your
very soul.

The dream had come to
pass in all of its lustre
to peace.

Unfortunately it would be gone
in a few hours
with only memories left.

Only ashes would remain.
The fire was so aggressive
that it ate everything in its
path, while it hungered for more.

The heat blazing beyond control
embers of sadness
across the forest floor.

Devastation, financial ruin
the dreamer
now on the brink.

Rebuilding was not an option.
The beauty destroyed.
The smells of cinders.
Dreams destroyed.

The fire now out, the
memories to share.

Some would have never
tried again.

Courage has a way of opening
new paths.
Be it adversity or
opportunity.

Broken dreams now held in
the hands.
The need for bread, the
heart psalm.

The wounds began to heal.
New direction called
defeat was but a moment.

Each day opportunity came
a new chance at success.
Back in the game.

Some time passed by, humility
the path.
But it was not long.
The millions came.

Lessons in life learned.
There were two fires that[95]
day.

The one they put out.
The one in his soul.
for success.[96] The flames
of the latter
increased from the loss.
The heat of passion
and success.
So did burn!

I find time to breathe, ponder, and reflect on

_____
_____
_____
_____
_____
_____
_____
_____
_____
_____
_____
_____

*I find time for love, joy, and
take time to write about*

_____
_____
_____
_____
_____
_____
_____
_____
_____
_____
_____
_____

*I take time to forgive and
release and write about*

_____
_____
_____
_____
_____
_____
_____
_____
_____
_____
_____

*I take time to respect and prioritize
my endeavors and write about*

_____
_____
_____
_____
_____
_____
_____
_____
_____
_____
_____
_____

45
Ship of Dreams

You could see the wrinkles
of years and time upon
his seafaring face. The
old captain had been upon
all the seas.[97]

Forced to retire, the military
day had come
with full honors.
Sadness filled his heart as
the tears
hid themselves
in his salty, wrinkled blue-
eyed face.

Sure, he enjoyed being home,
making memories with family.
But a land lover, he was not.[98]

Shortly after retiring, he found
himself in a different kind
of battle.
The visitor was cancer, a
new voyage
he would embark upon.
But his focus
was to get back to the sea.

He made changes in his
lifestyle,
worked to live and love longer.
Every day to the captain
had always been a gift.

As positivity and thought or
destiny can do,
he met a young dreamer,
an entrepreneur.

A treasure hunter who needed
the old captain,
his wisdom, his spirit.

Some years had passed by.
But it was time.

A plan was filed.
Now a dream was put
in motion.
A dreamer, the captain went
back to
the ocean.
This would be a short trip
for the old captain at best.

A few months went by. They
were met with success.
If you talk to the dreamer,
the entrepreneur,

here's what he would say,
"We were on our way back.
A terrible storm took us by
surprise, the wise and fearless
Captain would not leave the
helm, until we had reached safe waters.
Shortly after he knew
we were all safe, he passed
early morn.

"I had found more than I
had expected. What a cost.
I feared more the greeting
of his widow, Elizabeth, and his daughters.
As there was little joy now
in my heart.

"The days now passed slowly.
We arrived at port, I
felt my heart sink. I
could see Elizabeth now. I
prayed in my heart.
"The joy of all the other
shipmates, the sounds of
cheers flowed through the
salty air.

"Elizabeth walked up and gave
me a hug.
Then stepped back for a
moment of silence."

"Before you say anything, let
me share."
"She composed herself.
She was a strong lady.

She pulled out the letter,
then read.
I watched Elizabeth's tears
like dew from
heaven falling
to the pages
as she read.

She then looked into my
tear-filled eyes.
"You see,
his cancer had come
back.
He only had a few
months to live."
"The pain was real. We
both knew
he was the best
at sea. He
did rest."

Elizabeth said, "He was able to
do what his
heart did love."

"We hugged each other for
we both felt
him there.

"Do what you love.
Each day is
a gift.

A new ship he charts
An ocean where?
A spiritual voyage.
I know he's there.

I find time to breathe, ponder, and reflect on

_____
_____
_____
_____
_____
_____
_____
_____
_____
_____
_____

*I find time for love, joy, and
take time to write about*

_____
_____
_____
_____
_____
_____
_____
_____
_____
_____
_____

*I take time to forgive and
release and write about*

_____
_____
_____
_____
_____
_____
_____
_____
_____
_____
_____

*I take time to respect and prioritize
my endeavors and write about*

_____
_____
_____
_____
_____
_____
_____
_____
_____
_____
_____

46

Overcoming the Odds

She believes in
angels and miracles.
She believes we truly
find ourselves while
in the service of
others.[99]

Prior to her birth,
here upon Earth
her parents divorced,
her mother unstable,
her father estranged.

She would be raised
only a short time
by her mother.
Then a dozen
foster homes and
two group homes.
Relying on the
kindness of strangers.
She humbly tells me
she would not change a thing.
Paying it forward

in the service of others
does her heart sing.

Her parents who would
both be diagnosed with
terminal illnesses
in their darkest hours,
would find her by their side.[100]

She radiated with
forgiveness, kindness, and love.
Through her service
they could see and feel
her light.

With more teachers than
students for friends,
she believes she will be
forever learning.
In humility, she discusses her degrees.
She continues to study and serve
to no end.
Once again, she shares
with me
while walking by faith,
courage, strength,
her heart
sings.

She learned to play
multiple instruments.

Reading was her great escape.
Her art is found in
her daily work,
serving those
in need.

She works to
rescue children.
"How many," I asked?
"Several hundred," she replied.
All this while in the
service of others.

She believes in having
balance in her life.
She loves the outdoors.
The beauty of nature.
Time with family, her faith,
time to pray, time for yoga.
A heart of gratitude for each day.
A constant watch, she would say.

She has lost love.
She has found love.
Her children, her greatest joy.
A reverence for nature.
The sound of water.
The coo of a mourning dove.

She gently reminds me,
while walking by faith,

courage, and strength.
She has learned
we are never alone, and
she would not change a thing.

Through her example,
I am reminded
that our circumstances
do not define who we are
or who we become
but can propel each of us
to where we are meant to be.

She chooses the path of
victory
not victim.
That is the way you see!
The constant service of others
is the answer, again!
She wouldn't change a thing.

She would ask each of you
to do the same.
Start by serving, helping, and
saving the one.
And like her,
your greatest work may be yet
to be discovered.
Overcoming the odds.

I find time to breathe, ponder, and reflect on

_____
_____
_____
_____
_____
_____
_____
_____
_____
_____
_____

*I find time for love, joy, and
take time to write about*

_____
_____
_____
_____
_____
_____
_____
_____
_____
_____
_____

*I take time to forgive and
release and write about*

_____
_____
_____
_____
_____
_____
_____
_____
_____
_____
_____

*I take time to respect and prioritize
my endeavors and write about*

_____
_____
_____
_____
_____
_____
_____
_____
_____
_____
_____
_____

47
When Comes A Call

Jim called today.
Said he was concerned
about his friend.

I asked what I could
do.
He said
his friend needed many
prayers.

"What is your friend's name?"
I asked.
"Colby."
"What is the problem if it
is all right to ask?"[101]

"My friend is blind. I was
with him the other night
when he heard a song about
angels. He began to cry."
I was overcome. I tried
not to let Jim know

I was about to cry.

"Does this happen often?"

Jim replied, "Just when the song plays."
"Yes, Jim, I will do as you asked."

As I hung up the phone, I was caught up in the moment.
You see, Jim was born with half a lobe or, as doctors say, he is impaired.
Only one good leg and only one good arm.

But Jim always has a smile when I see him.
We always share a laugh or two.

Jim was not the least bit concerned for himself.
He just wanted his friend Colby
to be all right.[102]

I find time to breathe, ponder, and reflect on

_____
_____
_____
_____
_____
_____
_____
_____
_____
_____
_____
_____

*I find time for love, joy, and
take time to write about*

_____
_____
_____
_____
_____
_____
_____
_____
_____
_____
_____

*I take time to forgive and
release and write about*

_____
_____
_____
_____
_____
_____
_____
_____
_____
_____

*I take time to respect and prioritize
my endeavors and write about*

_____
_____
_____
_____
_____
_____
_____
_____
_____
_____
_____

48
Active Faith

I have met or known
individuals
who went to bed broke.
Storms do pass.
The sun does rise.
Insight and wisdom,
I now realize.

But they did believe.[103]

The next day followed.
By their belief,
a door was opened.
A miracle came.
Honest effort,
honest work
brought no shame.
Some even found fame.

But they did believe.
I have met some who
lost

all their possessions,
all their coins,
the very home that
gave them
shelter from the storms.

But they did believe.

Time brought fortune again.
With it came wisdom.
They said the wisdom
from the storms
brought character
so fortune
would be upon them.

But they did believe.

Friends suffered tragic
loss.
It would have thrown most
into the depths of despair.
More than most could
handle.
Few have been asked.

But they did believe.
Soon the storm clouds
passed.

Rays of sun did shine.
Joy, happiness, peace would return.
A warrior's heart to earn.

But they did believe.

Those individuals who lost
all hope
or love
while tears of sorrow came.
Enough moisture;
their own rain.[104]

But they did believe.

Love came when least expected.
Of course they were loved.
From on high,
hope returned.
With the smile
of grace.
With new vigor,
back in the race.
So when your trials do
come upon you,
remember those before you.

Others have overcome
more than words can say.
Live life, find solace this day.
It's time to believe.

I find time to breathe, ponder, and reflect on

_____
_____
_____
_____
_____
_____
_____
_____
_____
_____
_____

*I find time for love, joy, and
take time to write about*

_____
_____
_____
_____
_____
_____
_____
_____
_____
_____
_____

*I take time to forgive and
release and write about*

_____
_____
_____
_____
_____
_____
_____
_____
_____
_____

*I take time to respect and prioritize
my endeavors and write about*

_____
_____
_____
_____
_____
_____
_____
_____
_____
_____

49
The Other Side

What happens when a
father is asked to
become a coach of
his son's team?

Well, let's find out.
The father had never
been the head coach of
any of his childrens'
sports teams.

The father was a leader
in his chosen fields
but even he wondered
what he had gotten
himself into.

The son's faith in his
father,
the continued persistence
of the son,
opened the door of what

was to come.[105]

The son's father now
the head coach of
not just his son's
team but many other
sons and a daughter.

Soon into practice and
taking time to get to know
the parents and the players
this is how the story goes.

Two of the players were
adopted, yes the brothers
learned early on how to
look out for each other.

One of the players, the
only girl on the team
had just lost her father.
Keep reading, you will
soon see, she has a
warrior's heart, and the
courage of a lioness.

At the end of the first
two games of the season,
coach and players

were in a little dismay.
They had lost on both days.

After seeing each player's face,
something moved inside the coach.
Something said, "Finish the race."

Practice, input from assistants –
more practice –
helping each other
look out for one another.

Their next game, a win.
He would learn, each of
the players and
each of the families
were all going through something.

However, the players, families,
and coach were about to learn
from the young warriors, a
title they would earn.

Now the coach put his
heart and soul into
the game as he
watched the players and
families do the same.

With a few close calls,
a few more wins,
now deep into the season,
this group of players,
a band of warriors
continued to win.

Coach and families were
starting to see
this hopeful band of warriors
were so much more
than a team.

They had come together
to help their families
renew their spirit.
With each point,
the community
could hear it.

The young girl who
had recently laid her
father to rest
now had many brothers.

She would go on to
run and score.
Her warrior's heart
showed so much more.

The adopted brothers taught
the coach and others
how to look out
for each other.

When the season had
come to an end,
each had bonded,
the players and the
coach. Now spiritual warriors
would find themselves
playing against a team
they had lost to early
in the season.

Warming up in the early
morning rising sun.
With the smell of freshly cut grass.
In a few moments, they would
be on the field for game day,
for the championship, they would play.

Now a worthy opponent the
team faced.
Once again, the words
came to the coach.
"Finish the race."
At the end of the day,
this little band of warriors had won.

Then the coach
heard his son say,
"It's good to be on the other side."[106]
With cheers and handshakes,
the field began to clear.
Something incredible
happened here.
Something miraculous
happened that year.

I find time to breathe, ponder, and reflect on

_____
_____
_____
_____
_____
_____
_____
_____
_____
_____
_____

*I find time for love, joy, and
take time to write about*

_____
_____
_____
_____
_____
_____
_____
_____
_____
_____
_____

*I take time to forgive and
release and write about*

_____
_____
_____
_____
_____
_____
_____
_____
_____
_____
_____

*I take time to respect and prioritize
my endeavors and write about*

_____
_____
_____
_____
_____
_____
_____
_____
_____
_____
_____

50
There is a Season

Meditation will help you reach
your dreams.[107]
Prayers will open
doors.
Seeing is believing.

We have all heard one or
all of the above
positive affirmations.

Let me share a real life
experience of this.
Upon finishing my second book,
the manuscript ready for submission.

I wanted to have a captivating
review done, as every author
hopes for.
Or at least some
inspiring write up
for the back cover
before it was released.

I had access to a few
pro sports figures
as well as a few other
high-profile individuals.

Upon meditating and sincerely
praying about it, I kept
feeling I needed to be
patient, in
other words, "Peace, be still."

While the manuscript was in
final editing and review,
which felt like an eternity,
but was
only a few months,

I decided to go see a
movie at a local theater
with family and friends.

As I exited the theater, a very
nice looking, well-spoken
woman came up to me and
asked what I thought about
the movie.
I gave her an honest
answer, "I thought it was
great. I liked it." She

asked if I would share my
thoughts with her husband.

She went back into the
theater, came out with her
husband, and introduced
him to me. He was the
screenwriter of the movie
we had just watched. He
shared some thoughts with us,
shook our hands. Everyone
was smiling as a crowd
had gathered around.
Before leaving, he shook my hand
again and gave me his
card.
After a few emails, he
agreed to do a review of
my manuscript.

A few months later,
I received an amazing
respectable, "back-cover blurb"
with permission to use it.

It was more than I would
have ever asked for, more
than I anticipated.
Call it belief or prayer,[108]

I say both have a way
of delivering
even greater and more than
we anticipate if we can but
"peace be still" and listen.

Phil is a friend. The book
is titled *"Poetry for Peace."* His
kind words lifted my life.

Yes, meditation, visualization,
believing, and positive affirmations
do help.
I believe it was prayer that
helped our paths cross.

You call it what you will
but that's what
I believe.

Sure, I have had setbacks,
experienced loss.
But I keep doing.
I keep going.
This I do know:
dreams come true.
It happened for me, it can happen for you.

I find time to breathe, ponder, and reflect on

_____
_____
_____
_____
_____
_____
_____
_____
_____
_____
_____
_____

*I find time for love, joy, and
take time to write about*

_____
_____
_____
_____
_____
_____
_____
_____
_____
_____
_____
_____

*I take time to forgive and
release and write about*

_____
_____
_____
_____
_____
_____
_____
_____
_____
_____

*I take time to respect and prioritize
my endeavors and write about*

_____
_____
_____
_____
_____
_____
_____
_____
_____
_____

51
Righteous Among Nations

When do we find our
life's work?
May I submit that most
of the events
lead us there if we are
but open to the path?[109]

A young man whose father
was a doctor had the
way and educational honors
so that he could become
a doctor too.

But his heart, the times he
lived in had a different
path.

He would become a diplomat
during a time of great
conflicts and war.
I might note he would
have brought less risk to

his family as well
as himself, by following
in his father's
footsteps.

What the heart wants,
it wants.

So the journey began to
an outpost in a desolated
area.

He was to issue temporary
visas
to those who qualified.

But found himself working
well beyond the normal
demands of the position.

He made choices based on
what was right, not on
business as usual.

This would come at a cost
of personal sacrifice as well
as safety.
Over an estimated three
month period, he would

help thousands of war-torn refugees
on their journey to safer places.

Recently, I read that because
of his selfless acts, there
are thousands of
descendants alive
today.

Yes, a price was paid.

As I read of the ordinary
individual[110]
who achieved extraordinary things
in his life
by rising to give hope,
freedom, and life
to those around him,

I could not help but
ponder or wonder
what greatness comes
if we but follow our
heart?
Our life's work
is limitless
if we follow
the path.
How many lives can you
impact?

How many descendants will
be here
because of you?

What impact may you have
even if it's upon
one other
or yourself?

What is your heart asking
of you?
If it be a righteous
path,
pursue.

A diplomat but a title
humanitarian, yes.
Freedom given
hope to many.[110]
The right thing.
Music of his heart.
He listened and
many now sing.

Oh, yes because many now
sing.

I find time to breathe, ponder, and reflect on

_____
_____
_____
_____
_____
_____
_____
_____
_____
_____
_____

*I find time for love, joy, and
take time to write about*

_____
_____
_____
_____
_____
_____
_____
_____
_____
_____
_____

*I take time to forgive and
release and write about*

_____
_____
_____
_____
_____
_____
_____
_____
_____
_____

*I take time to respect and prioritize
my endeavors and write about*

_____
_____
_____
_____
_____
_____
_____
_____
_____
_____
_____

52
On Bended Knee

As an orphan he used to
ride the trains.
His father was shot
then left for dead.

While in the military, his
company was hit so
hard
that out of 252, he was
one of only
36 that
survived.[111]

He spent months in
the military
hospital
recovering
from the bullet wounds
and shrapnel.
Later he married
his sweetheart
but was tried
again.

As they buried his
third child.
His name was Doug.

This would have broken
most people
I know.

Then a few years later,
he lost
his sweetheart.
To the
depths of sorrow
he
sank.

Fortune prior had shined
upon him
as he was
blessed
with four treasures:
his children.
A great
reason
to live.
As the darkness followed,
soon did the
light.
He often shared

with prayer
that it would be all right.

A *Warrior,* a hero who
survives
the fight
as quoted
with prayer it will be
all right.

He focused on his dreams.
He followed his
heart.

Made great contributions
in his chosen field.
His so-called
art.

Many would have quit. How
easy
it would
have been.
Warriors carry on,
with courage to stand.

The dreams came true, he
finished the
race.

And he sat with the
nobles
but was humble, sometimes
meek.

Charity he practiced. People
he helped.
A warrior inside.
A friend
of mine.

When all is stacked against
you,
or the road is too
hard,
remember the
spiritual warrior
who followed his heart.[112]

I find time to breathe, ponder, and reflect on

_____
_____
_____
_____
_____
_____
_____
_____
_____
_____
_____
_____

*I find time for love, joy, and
take time to write about*

_____
_____
_____
_____
_____
_____
_____
_____
_____
_____
_____

*I take time to forgive and
release and write about*

_____
_____
_____
_____
_____
_____
_____
_____
_____
_____

*I take time to respect and prioritize
my endeavors and write about*

_____
_____
_____
_____
_____
_____
_____
_____
_____
_____

Afterword

Let us be mindful of...

The man who didn't read or write
until his late teens, and who later becomes
a university professor.

Let us be mindful of...

The soldier who honorably served
and sacrificed his ability to
walk, only to rise again
and win by being a great
husband, father, and winner of
a Paralympic medal.

Let us be mindful of...

The musician who came from
an abusive, poverty-stricken
situation, to become a best-
selling songwriter and
a multiplatinum artist who
uses their status to lift up
and help others.

Let us be mindful of...

The single parent who works
two or more jobs so their
children can go to great
trade schools, colleges, or universities.

Let us be mindful of...

The abused child or spouse
who rises above to help
free those in similar
situations.

Let us be mindful of...

The terminal patient who
brings their therapy pet
into the clinics and hospitals
to help relieve the suffering
of others.

Let us be mindful of...

The child who loses a
parent to an illness and
grows up and becomes a
healthcare professional
who provides care to patients
who so desperately need it.

Let us be mindful of…

The pro sports athlete who
is injured so as to never
play again, then later
becomes one of the greatest
coaches of their generation.

Let us be mindful of…

The child who was in and
out of multiple homes,
homeless and in and out
of various schools – only to
grow up to become an
educator, a principal, a mentor.
Having her school become distinguished,
working with her staff to see her
students find their greatness.

Let us be mindful of…

Those with impairments
or disabilities who go on to help
others and make a mark
with patents,
new technologies, medical breakthroughs,
and a host of other
contributions to the humanities.

Let us be mindful of...

Those who have found a
path that makes life
and the world a little
better for each of us.

Let us be mindful of...

The humanitarian who
went through homelessness and
hunger, to rise up and
help house and feed
those in need by using
the foundation they and their
team built as a platform to
leave a legacy.

Acknowledgments

A huge blessing of gratitude for my touchstone parents, Julia, Fern, Elaine, and George for a lifetime of love and support, for reading and sharing adventures, art, great books, and music with me. And for their insightful guidance and direction along with the other villagers.

Eternal love for my wife and children for their infinite love, encouragement, inspiration, and strength. They humble me every day and never cease to make me proud with the way they use their gifts.

To the artists, mentors, teachers, counselors, healers, therapists, and yogis who invest in others and make a difference for good while on this journey called life.

To my publisher for believing in me and shepherding this book through many incarnations, while never losing sight of the ultimate goal.

To my tireless publicist for her dedication and resolve and for keeping me on my toes and on target.

To those inspirational poets – both past and present – those philosophers of the written word who teach and practice wholeness, wellness, and balance. Those gifted with the power of finding and creating peace through poetry are true blessings whom we can look to for the spirit of healing.

My humble gratitude also to David Tate, PhD, who encouraged and helped, guide, and inspire me to turn this book into an interactive workbook that could benefit others.

To the brave and courageous souls who shared just a few of their experiences and examples of courage, faith, and a miracle or two along the path of rescuing.

And to my indispensable editor, Kristen Weber, who took my writings and found within them further inspiration, shaping this interactive book into the valuable road map it has become.

Above all, many thanks to our infinite Creator and His Son, our master healers, who teach us that with patience, self-reflection, and the fervent desire to do better, we can achieve true peace.

About the Author

The son of a Bronze Star and Purple Heart Soldier who was killed in action when K.S. was four, K.S. Dwyer is a military Gold Star son and family member who comes from humble beginnings.

He recognized early in life the importance of having great mentors and learning from great teachers, and does everything he can to mentor and serve others. Throughout his career, K.S. has been an entrepreneur and a business magnate for a variety of companies including bootstrap start-ups, public and private organizations in the education, entertainment, professional sports, and financial fields. He has been involved in mergers and acquisitions, and has a deep belief in philanthropy, including working with a multitude of charitable organizations.

K.S. has long believed in community and ecclesiastical service, and in all he does, he seeks solace and wisdom.

Having served at various times as co-founder, president, CEO, and Chairman of the Board for several companies, K.S. has never forgotten the importance of being associated with gifted individuals in all facets of life. A firm believer in the words of Winston Churchill, "Success is not final; failure is not fatal: it is the courage to continue that counts," K.S. believes that both success and failure give us the opportunity to gain knowledge and wisdom, as well as a chance to grow. When not working or writing, K.S. spends time with his family at the ocean, boarding in a kaleidoscopic barrel wave, boating, biking, horseback riding, or contemplating the rhythms of life at a baseball game – one of the places he considers to be a house of hope and healing. K.S. also enjoys exploration – especially of islands or mountains – or any place where he can be at one with nature. He appreciates the adventure of the outdoors and the smell of flowers and fresh air.

Poems for Courage is the latest book by K.S. Dwyer. For more information about his previous books, please visit his website at www.ksdwyer.com

Sources

1. A Taste of Coastal Bliss

1. There is evidence to suggest that living near – or spending time close to – the sea is good for one's mental health. There is science that confirms that sea water and salty sea air is good for us, physically, but there is also a calming mental effect of proximity to the ocean. Perhaps it is because of the calming, rhythmic nature of the waves or the sea breeze, but either way, people who spend more time closer to the ocean, tend to report fewer mental health issues. https://www.vogue.co.uk/beauty/article/sea-for-mental-health

2. Likewise, having a "healthy relationship with chocolate" can be a benefit to our health as well. Similarly, chocolate contains antioxidants, which can promote heart health. But beyond that, often eating or drinking chocolate makes people happy, and happy people tend to be less stressed. https://www.hopkinsmedicine.org/health/wellness-and-prevention/the-benefits-of-having-a-healthy-relationship-with-chocolate#:~:text=Increases%20heart%20health%3A%20The%20antioxidants,and%20death%20from%20heart%20disease.

2. God's Willing Hand

3. Courage is one of, if not the most important qualities necessary for enlisting. However, planting the seeds of courage starts much earlier: https://www.armyandnavyacademy.org/blog/courage-is-key-to-being-prepared-for-an-unsure-future/

4. The B-17 Flying Fortress is one of the most famous aircraft in history. https://amcmuseum.org/at-the-museum/aircraft/b-17g-flying-fortress/

5. There are countless stories of soldiers reporting seeing angels on the battlefield. One of the most famous is the account of the "Angels of Mons" reported by British soldiers in World War I. https://warfarehistorynetwork.com/article/world-war-i-miracle-the-angels-of-mons/

6. There are no shortage of stories of the courage of POWs. Army Air Forces Sergeant Lloyd Ponder shares his story and speaks about the power of hope, and how hope can lead to courage. https://www.af.mil/News/Article-Display/Article/1393369/world-war-ii-pow-survivor-shares-tale-of-hope-determination-resilience/

7. Given the high prices often paid for joining the military, it would stand to reason that many people would have regrets about their choices. However, the opposite is true. Veterans who served in Iraq and Afghanistan

overwhelmingly support their decisions in retrospect. This is perhaps surprising because more modern veterans are generally not afforded the same respect as veterans from previous generations, such as those who served in World War II. https://www.washingtonpost.com/news/post-nation/wp/2014/04/08/few-regrets-89-of-iraq-and-afghanistan-vets-would-do-it-all-over-again/

3. Seeds of Greatness

8. Making a difference can seem like an impossible ask when we consider all the things that need to be fixed in the world today. However, as with any type of success, if we break this task down into small, actionable goals, we will find that making a difference is easier than we think. https://tinybuddha.com/blog/25-ways-to-make-a-difference-in-the-world-every-day/

9. One of the most difficult things to do is to be courageous, yet one of the easiest things to do is to encourage others. Fill others with courage by supporting, loving, and understanding them. https://leadershipfreak.blog/2011/12/21/five-ways-to-fill-others-with-courage/

4. A Ray of Hope

10. Mahatma Gandhi famously said, "There is enough for everyone's need, but not for everyone's greed." This truism is constantly being tested and we are learning that in order to provide for all, we need to work towards equity and economic stabilization. https://www.thenationalnews.com/opinion/comment/the-earth-provides-enough-to-meet-everyone-s-needs-1.426562

11. There is a fascinating study about whether guilt is a useful motivator in getting people to do the right thing. The concept of "reparative action" states that people feel guilty for doing (or not doing) something and so therefore are motivated to "make things right" by taking corrective action. For example, if someone feels guilty for not eating vegetarian, perhaps they will donate to an animal rescue charity. There is also a difference between internal guilt and external guilt. It has been proven that external guilt – or trying to make someone feel guilty for something, tends to cause defensiveness and rationalization, not change. https://psyche.co/ideas/you-want-people-to-do-the-right-thing-save-them-the-guilt-trip

5. I Do See

12. Feeding our emotional needs is more difficult than taking care of physical hunger, but no less important. Understanding ourselves and the ways in which we need emotional sustenance can help us become more in tune with our own needs and therefore, can make us better able to address the emotional needs of others. https://medium.com/swlh/are-you-feeding-your-emotional-needs-fbb5e22e3274

13. True growth comes from being able to see beyond ourselves. In most cases, this is an intentional decision that takes work and practice. https://medium.com/@NataliMorad/how-do-we-grow-by-reaching-beyond-ourselves-fc7deef2e308#:~:text=Reaching%20beyond%20yourself%20means%20having,prove%20that%20you%20are%20right.

6. A Mother's Loving Prayer

14. There is evidence to suggest that there is a strong correlation between parents and their ability to feel their children's pain. There are interesting differences between fathers and mothers and how they experience their children's pain. https://www.ncbi.nlm.nih.gov/pmc/articles/PMC3105525/#:~:text=Parent%2Dchild%20pain%20relationships%3A%20Quantitative,47%25%20of%20mothers%20of%20boys.

15. The weight carried by mothers is nearly staggering – and yet mothers are the strongest among us. https://www.scarymommy.com/motherhood-heaviness

16. Meditation can be a powerful tool to help fight insomnia or to lead to better sleep, even without pre-existing sleep problems. https://www.sleepfoundation.org/insomnia/treatment/meditation

17. Making friends as we grow older becomes more and more difficult. One of the biggest things we can do to grow our circle of friends is to overcome the fear of rejection. Courage is necessary. There are also other tactics we can employ to grow adult friendship. https://tinybuddha.com/blog/11-ways-to-turn-strangers-into-friends/

7. I Am

18. The concept of sensory memory relates to how the senses – smell, touch, taste, hearing, and sight – can trigger memories for us. Some sensory memories, when experienced during a period of mourning, can be incredibly powerful. https://www.simplypsychology.org/sensory-memory.html

19. In Jewish custom, when someone has died, it is customary to say "May their memory be a blessing," which speaks to the carrying on of memory. As there is no Jewish conception of the afterlife (at least not a universal and agreed upon one), the idea that memories outlast people is a powerful one. https://reformjudaism.org/learning/answers-jewish-questions/what-jewish-expression-refer-someone-who-has-died

8. Answering the Call

20. Reconnecting with old friends can be difficult, and in some cases, fraught, especially if there were difficult circumstances or if the friendship

occurred during a difficult time in your life of which you do not wish to be reminded. But this reconnection can also be good for the soul. https://secondwindmovement.com/reconnect-old-friends/

21. We all know that listening is important. There have been studies conducted on just this topic. This one in particular focuses on a nurse in a medical setting who lost her voice and discovered that her communication with her patients actually improved when she could not speak to them. There is a similar idea at work in talk therapy. Listening is incredibly powerful. https://www.magonlinelibrary.com/doi/abs/10.12968/bjon.1997.6.5.275

9. Top of the Mountain

22. We're not imagining it; we are all our own worst critics and need to give ourselves more grace. https://www.theguardian.com/science/2018/apr/14/ellen-hendriksen-we-are-each-our-own-worst-critic-social-anxiety-disorder-interview

23. "Footprints in the Sand" is a popular allegorical poem on similar themes. https://en.wikipedia.org/wiki/Footprints_(poem)

10. It Will Be All Right

24. The temptation to give up is human and real. Choosing not to takes courage. One of the most important things we can do when times are bad is to allow ourselves to acknowledge and feel the misfortune. Not allowing ourselves to mourn what was lost will only lead to setbacks. We must experience the full range of emotions if we are to dig ourselves out of the hole. https://www.inc.com/andrew-thomas/10-things-that-will-help-you-keep-going-when-times-get-tough.html

25. Our lives are complex and difficult. We can be helped by attempting to see the world through the eyes of a child. Sometimes, all we need is to strip away the trappings and concerns of the larger adult world and realize that, like a child believes, everything will be all right. https://www.huffpost.com/entry/seeing-the-world-through_b_13784800

11. The Gift of Freedom

26. American freedom is a precious and complex thing. We are taught of the sacrifices others made so that we can enjoy freedom, but what we don't often consider is that freedom is not a static thing. We are still fighting for it every day. Freedom is a complex web with many layers that must be examined carefully. https://en.wikipedia.org/wiki/Real_freedom

27. The Library of Congress has compiled many poems of thanks written to veterans. They are powerful and moving. https://www.loc.gov/programs/

poetry-and-literature/poet-laureate/poet-laureate-projects/la-casa-de-colores/la-familia/item/poetry-00000194/thank-you-poems-to-our-vets/

12. In the Moment

28. Self-reflection is a crucial part of true happiness. Don't forget to reflect regularly on yourself and your life. Doing so allows us to see things we might otherwise gloss over in the haste of life. https://www.chrisistace.com/the-importance-of-self-reflection-and-happiness/

29. We can thank the universe for all that we have, all that we are, and all that we may become. Whatever your faith background, there are reasons for gratitude. https://www.joincake.com/blog/how-to-thank-the-universe/

13. On the Ropes

30. There is an argument to be made that letting others win sometimes benefits us all. https://vishalsarang.com/when-and-why-you-should-let-others-win/

31. There is great courage in losing. It is difficult and can negatively affect our perception of ourselves. If we let it. https://medium.com/the-ascent/having-the-courage-to-lose-a02781c2beeb

14. Of the Heart

32. Did you know there is an actual day to practice and celebrate random acts of kindness? It's February 17 and here are some ways to partake: https://www.good-deeds-day.org/10-random-acts-of-kindness-for-rak-day/?gclid=CjwKCAiAs8acBhA1EiwAgRFdw-Iaf1y0-sZoES4NZ2S5JyLFz6QKXIrdjKr4kPbwM1GOyAmv5oDeBxoC57QQAvD_BwE

33. Truly, money can't buy happiness, but it can buy things to make our lives easier. And yet, there are real studies to suggest that wealthy people are not the happiest. https://hbr.org/2016/06/why-rich-people-arent-as-happy-as-they-could-be

15. True Friendship

34. Friends, especially true friends, are crucially important to living fulfilling lives. Friends hold value for us in so many ways. https://glenora.net/the-value-of-friendship/#:~:text=Good%20friends%20are%20vitally%20important,the%20full%20experience%20of%20life.

35. Lifelong friendships are perhaps more rare than we imagine. There are certain traits that are common among people that have been friends for

many, many years. Mostly, these relationships are additive, and they do not stress the parties involved. We want our friends to add to our lives, not pull focus from them. Friends support us – as we support them. https://www.flashpack.com/us/solo/relationships/surprising-trait-lifelong-friend/

16. Duty to Lift Up

36. In the television show *The Good Place*, there is an underlying current about relational morality based on T.M. Scanlon's theory that we all owe something to each other. The Episode "What We Owe To Each Other" does an excellent job of tackling this question in a humorous way. https://thegoodplace.fandom.com/wiki/Chapter_6:_What_We_Owe_to_Each_Other

37. Serving and helping others is not an entirely altruistic act. It actually makes us feel good too! https://www.operationinasmuch.org/blog/why-we-feel-good-when-we-serve/?gclid=CjwKCAiAs8acBhA1EiwAgRFdw1CoOq0YrLuLNPH14dOSu-_8qwVG_wXQ_mra4Tz39eAsvyjuILCVURoC6pMQAvD_BwE

17. Inner Strength

38. A shift in perspective can also mean a shift for success. Redefining what success looks like for us can make all the difference. https://www.minimalismmadesimple.com/home/change-perspective/

39. There is evidence to suggest that initial failure leads people to be even more determined and may be a driver for success. Many, many, many people throughout history have failed several times before succeeding. https://www.inc.com/scott-mautz/11-famous-failures-that-will-inspire-you-to-succes.html#:~:text=Henry%20Ford's%20first%20two%20automobile,the%20first%20working%20Dyson%20vacuum

18. By My Side

40. You've heard the phrase "winning isn't everything." There is some truth to that. Losing may, in fact, be better for us in the long run because we learn more through challenge than we do from success. https://gladiatorguards.com/winning-isnt-everything-sometimes-its-good-to-lose/#:~:text=So%20if%20winning%20is%20so,bad%20habits%20begin%20to%20develop.

41. Of course we know that coaches teach players, but it's possible that players teach coaches – and have an even bigger impact on their lives. https://footballscoop.com/news/5-lessons-coaches-tend-learn-players

19. Take That First Step

42. Jim Abbott was a professional baseball player who had a pitching career that spanned ten years, despite being born without a right hand. https://en.wikipedia.org/wiki/Jim_Abbott
43. Sports, in particular, is full of extraordinary stories of people who have had to overcome physical hardships to achieve greatness. Their stories are inspiring. https://www.history.com/news/11-olympians-who-overcame-disabilities

20. It Matters to Me

44. There are studies that show that those with less means are actually more charitable than the wealthy. There are many reasons for why this might be but one of them is the belief that those with less might have more empathy for the situations people find themselves in and may better understand the value of charitable giving. https://www.npr.org/templates/story/story.php?storyId=129068241

45. There is an argument to be made that a donation made by someone with very little means more than a donation made by a wealthy person, because there is more effort and more sacrifice involved in making the donation. https://philanthropynewsdigest.org/news/poor-americans-are-country-s-most-charitable-demographic

21. Rekindle Your Dreams

46. Children are wiser than we give them credit for. We tend to believe that wisdom comes only with experience, but perhaps it's less experience and more the ability to see the world without the veil of disappointment and darkness. https://mashable.com/ad/article/wise-kids-advice

47. We are taught that we should be positive towards our children and praise them when they do well. However, research suggests that encouragement is more important than praise. Encouragement acknowledges effort, regardless of outcome. Praise can backfire and can lead children to have perfectionist tendencies and to be hard on themselves. Encouragement allows them to know that it doesn't matter how they perform, but that they try, and children who are not afraid to try can accomplish great things. https://childcare.extension.org/encouragement-is-more-effective-than-praise-in-guiding-childrens-behavior/

22. Courage to Stand

48. There is a whole field of study related to near death experiences and the effect they can have on humans mentally, physically, and spiritually. https://

med.virginia.edu/perceptual-studies/our-research/near-death-experiences-ndes/

49. There is a belief that shared pain – or trauma – can bring people together. Experiments have been conducted to test this but it stands to reason that going through a traumatic experience would bring you closer to someone else who has experienced the same thing because of the unique nature of that experience. Explaining trauma to those who have not experienced it is difficult. It is that inherent bond that can bring people closer together. https://www.psychologicalscience.org/news/releases/shared-pain-brings-people-together.html

23. We All Matter

50. The Beatitudes are a cornerstone of Christian faith, describing how those who experience misfortune will be blessed. The common understanding is that in Christian faith, no one is forgotten, not even those who are suffering. https://en.wikipedia.org/wiki/Beatitudes

51. There is a beautiful quote from the naturalist, John Muir: "The sun shines not on us but in us." This is a helpful way of thinking of our place in the world. We are both integral and insignificant. https://vault.sierraclub.org/john_muir_exhibit/writings/mountain_thoughts.aspx

24. Here With Me

52. Whether or not guardian angels exist, many people believe they do, and that may be more important. https://abcnews.go.com/US/guardian-angels-exist-investigating-invisible-companions/story?id=19053535

53. Good Samaritans may, in fact, be "angels in temporal form." https://en.wikipedia.org/wiki/Parable_of_the_Good_Samaritan

25. A Time To Rise Up

54. Potential is not prescriptive, it does not come from outside of us. Instead, potential is something that is within us. And therefore, we get to define its limits. Simply because someone else has declared that you are not living up to your potential does not make it true. You are the one who defines what you are capable of. https://www.lifehack.org/articles/productivity/15-signs-you-are-living-your-potential-though-you-dont-know-you-are.html

55. Potential and promise are synonyms. It is important to understand that discovering your true potential may be a lifelong process. Decoupling potential from the hustle mindset is also difficult. A frank self-assessment can help you determine what you are capable of. https://www.lifehack.org/884917/understanding-your-potential

26. Opportunity in Adversity

56. This is a fascinating discussion about why bad things happen and how we can impose meaning on them once they occur. https://www.psychologytoday.com/us/blog/finding-purpose/201910/why-do-bad-things-happen-good-people

57. It stands to reason that depression is an outcome of personal failure, but there have been studies conducted about whether or not rumination on failure – that is thinking about it – leads to prolonged periods of depression. It appears there is a delicate balance between self-reflection and rumination. https://www.ncbi.nlm.nih.gov/pmc/articles/PMC3864849/

27. Nurtured By Nature

58. Helping others to heal is incredibly helpful in our own evolution of healing. It's almost magical in that making someone else feel better makes us feel better as well. Often that's because the act of helping someone to heal takes our focus off ourselves, which is sorely needed. https://lisaappelo.com/when-helping-others-is-healing-to-ourselves/

59. Emotional healing is just as, if not more important than physical healing, but it can be much harder to do because our emotions are hidden. It can be difficult to tell if someone is suffering emotionally. In order to work towards healing ourselves emotionally, there are concrete steps we can take. We can be physically perfect, but unless we are emotionally healthy, we will never be whole. https://www.psychologytoday.com/us/blog/rethinking-mental-health/201309/10-tips-emotional-healing

28. More Valuable Than Gold

60. Though the parable of the Good Samaritan is ubiquitous, in practice, the picture is far more bleak. We have become a country of inward thinking and self-concerned people, unwilling to help others in crisis. We must do better. https://www.dailymail.co.uk/sciencetech/article-3546439/The-good-Samaritan-dying-America-Just-one-39-people-help-strangers-medical-emergency.html

61. There is evidence to suggest that "paying it forward" is a deeply transformative act that can lead to happiness, connection, and community. https://greatergood.berkeley.edu/article/item/pay_it_forward

29. Those Who Believe

62. There is fascinating research being conducted on whether or not the actively religious – or spiritual – are healthier and happier than those people

who do not subscribe to or follow a system of religion or faith. Results, like people, are complex. https://www.pewresearch.org/fact-tank/2019/01/31/are-religious-people-happier-healthier-our-new-global-study-explores-this-question/

63. It is a false dichotomy to claim that the faithful cannot be scientific and vice versa. There is no competition between science and faith. Medieval Jewish philosopher Maimonides wrote extensively about the concept of miracles and the "unmoved mover." https://www.jstor.org/stable/23506857

30. Your Truth

64. It is important to remember that our words matter less than our actions when defining us. Intention is not as important as impact. We must make sure that our actions reflect the kind of people we truly are. https://exploringyourmind.com/actions-define-us-not-words/

65. There are few things that are near universal in all faith cultures, but the concept of good deeds is one of them. The motivation for such good deeds varies but the central tenet is there. https://www.pinalcentral.com/religion/good-deeds-not-particular-to-one-religion/article_04b3b21f-39bd-534c-a8ac-dbd71dfc84a3.html

31. Angels' Landing

66. Angels' Landing is a truly breathtaking site in Zion National Park, and one of the author's favorite places. https://www.visitutah.com/places-to-go/parks-outdoors/zion/outdoor-experiences/angels-landing

67. In our increasingly individualistic world, asking for help is one of the most courageous things we can do. Thankfully, people generally want to help. We must be open to both giving help when asked and be humble enough to ask for help when we need it. https://emindful.com/2020/05/21/2020-05-21-how-to-ask-for-help/

68. French philosopher Pierre Teilhard de Chardin once said, "We are not human beings having a spiritual experience. WE are spiritual beings having a human experience." These experiences are often more easily felt in some awe-inspiring places in nature, and understanding them is key to good mental health: https://basicsteps.life/2023/03/spiritual-beings-having-a-human-experience/

32. Breaking the Chains

69. One need not look far to see inspirational stories of successful people who have managed to overcome near-insurmountable odds to achieve greatness. https://www.huffpost.com/entry/successful-people-

obstacles_n_3964459

70. The concept of perseverance – or grit – is a fascinating one and one that has been studied at length. Can it be taught? And how? https://singjupost.com/true-grit-can-perseverance-be-taught-by-angela-lee-duckworth-transcript/

71. Anthropologist Margaret Mead famously said, "Never doubt that a small group of thoughtful, committed citizens can change the world. Indeed, it is the only thing that ever has." The same can be said of a single individual determined to make a difference. https://amysmartgirls.com/the-power-of-one-is-the-theory-that-one-person-can-change-the-future-that-one-person-s-actions-c058054689b0

33. Blue Coast Courage

72. Many people who surf approach it more like a religion than a pastime. There is some research about the reverence people feel being at one with the water. https://www.theatlantic.com/entertainment/archive/2017/07/is-surfing-more-religion-than-sport/533721/

73. Not panicking during a wipeout is one of the most important things you can do to ensure your safety. https://morganismyname.com/how-not-to-panic-during-a-wipeout-four-tips-to-help-you-stay-calm-when-you-are-caught-inside-or-in-a-hold-down/

34. The Path of Giants

74. Individualism – while highly prized – has its pitfalls. The ambition for personal gain and achievement can lead to competition and then anxiety. Collective striving can lighten one's personal load and the pressure one puts on oneself. https://www.ncbi.nlm.nih.gov/pmc/articles/PMC3942875/#:~:text=In%20particular%2C%20individualistic%20systems%20urge,et%20al.%2C%202013).

75. Mentors can be incredibly valuable and helpful. They can enrich our personal, professional, and spiritual lives. https://chronus.com/blog/why-mentoring-matters

35. You Have Purpose

76. Too often we consider adversity to be a challenge, a stumbling block in our path. However, there is value in reframing this and learning to welcome adversity as an opportunity to achieve. https://sakhashree.com/why-you-must-welcome-adversity/

77. We've all heard the saying "what doesn't kill you, makes you stronger."

There is some truth to that. In adversity, we are often forced to be creative and inventive, which can lead to greater accomplishments than we previously considered. https://medium.com/the-mission/adversity-leads-to-greatness-so-you-can-overcome-your-limitations-86a783d7e7e4

36. Inspirational Drive

78. Aaron Wheelz Fotheringham is known as the "godfather of extreme wheelchair sports" and has done some truly incredible things. https://www.youtube.com/watch?v=GYsMvWC67uM

79. Despite how we are told time and time again to aim higher, strive for more, and push ourselves, there is also freedom in accepting our limitations. As with facing adversity, limitations can often lead to creative solutions and accomplishments we didn't previously envision. https://www.psychologytoday.com/us/blog/evolution-the-self/201707/yes-you-can-t-why-you-should-affirm-your-limitations

37. Beyond the Hunger

80. Aside from parents – and in some cases instead of parents – siblings can be the most important people in our lives. An exploration of the ways in which siblings impact our lives is a fascinating one. https://singjupost.com/jeff-kluger-the-hidden-power-of-siblings-at-tedxasheville-transcript/

81. Parentification, or the act of an older sibling raising younger siblings, has many emotional and long-term effects on everyone involved. https://www.parents.com/parenting/better-parenting/i-parented-my-sibling-as-a-child-and-heres-how-it-changed-my-life/

38. In Honor Of

82. Childhood friendships are among the most important we will make. This is largely because those friendships are the ones we make when we are learning to be multi-faceted humans operating within a community and a society. https://bloomcharity.org/the-importance-of-childhood-friendships/#:~:text=Through%20childhood%20friendships%2C%20children%20learn,is%20experiencing%20a%20particular%20feeling.

83. Grief is a complicated thing, grieving even more so. For some people, grieving can be a lifelong process in which we are pushed to accomplish more as a way to psychologically "make up" for our loss. https://www.npr.org/sections/health-shots/2021/12/20/1056741090/grief-loss-holiday-brain-healing

39. Forty-five Cents

84. Success can be defined in any number of ways, but what's most important is understanding that you are the only person who can define success for yourself. https://soulsalt.com/what-does-success-mean/

85. Success is a process, not a destination. This is important to remember in that we have never achieved everything we will ever achieve. We can always strive for more, while being aware that we can be content with what we have. It's a delicate balance. https://medium.com/@tlxreed/success-is-a-process-not-a-destination-3551ac63a1bf

40. Why Not You?

86. The numbers change depending on the type of business one wishes to start, but the amounts are generally less than you likely think. https://www.businessnewsdaily.com/5-small-business-start-up-costs-options.html

87. It can be good practice for us to try to view the world as a child would. If we can let our inhibitions and adult concerns go, even for a little while, we may feel the freedom of being children again. https://wallstreetinsanity.com/9-reasons-why-you-should-view-the-world-through-a-childs-eyes/

41. In the Service of Others

88. There is a crucial difference between being hungry and starving. It's important to understand the difference and how best to combat each one. https://indianexpress.com/article/lifestyle/health/starve-and-hunger-know-the-difference-7994713/#:~:text=%E2%80%9CHunger%20is%20the%20feeling%20of,because%20your%20body%20needs%20food.

89. Taking calculated risks – especially as children – can have a huge impact on the kinds of risks we take as adults. It's important to know that we have support as we take risks but that we must also be aware of the potential consequences. https://www.inlander.com/spokane/calculated-risks-help-kids-gain-confidence-and-wisdom/Content?oid=18084240

42. A Mother's Love

90. It's not our imagination. The bond between a mother and a daughter is among the strongest there is. https://www.kidspot.com.au/parenting/study-finds-motherdaughter-bond-is-stronger-than-any-other/news-story/e645a8460f6e0f741af56c2fa4e11df0

91. We don't have to go far to find stories of mothers who have fought for their children, both physically and otherwise. Mothers are truly superheroes.

https://www.womansday.com/life/real-women/a1522/moms-whove-risked-it-all-to-save-their-kids-106576/

43. Your Mind

92. Teachers have a gift. The good ones are basically teaching magic. https://freedomtoteach.collins.co.uk/are-teachers-basically-magic-weavers/

93. Teachers are remarkable. But great teachers are truly life-changing. What do great teachers do better than others? https://www.educationworld.com/a_curr/what-great-teachers-do-differently.shtml#:~:text=Genuine%20caring%20and%20kindness%3B,learning%20opportunities%20for%20students%3B%20and

44. From the Ashes

94. Residents of Montana are pushing for a conservation trust to preserve some of the natural landscape for animal habitats. https://helenair.com/news/state-and-regional/govt-and-politics/coalition-proposes-montana-conservation-trust-fund/article_1f95383e-a274-5484-912d-1288157bcff5.html

95. Forest fires, while devastating, can also be beneficial to encouraging new growth and biodiversity. https://twbwf.org/fire-friend-or-foe-part-1/?gclid=Cj0KCQiA1sucBhDgARIsAFoytUvzDLEoy32Gs_GwUR-YcMidXopPILnpJ9T4fJyXVA8hsgRHVULUCDIaAt5bEALw_wcB

96. A burning desire for success is a great indicator that you will become successful. Just make sure you're cultivating your burning desire in the best way: https://www.depthnotwidth.com/your-burning-desire-a-powerful-predictor-of-success-and-failure/

45. Ship of Dreams

97. Read more about this particular story in the author's full-length work, *Pearls for Prosperity*. https://www.amazon.com/Pearls-Prosperity-Journey-Wealth-Dwyer/dp/1432786008

98. Salt air is good for us! https://selectsalt.com/halotherapy-blog/is-breathing-salt-air-good-for-you/#:~:text=The%20detoxifying%20effects%20of%20breathing,being%20and%20quality%20of%20life

46. Overcoming the Odds

99. Lots of people do good for a lot of reasons. What does it mean to be a do gooder and how can we become one? https://averageadvocate.

com/2015/08/what-are-do-gooders-do-gooders-definition/

100. There is research to support the theory that childhood trauma can lead to increased empathy in adulthood. https://www.ncbi.nlm.nih.gov/pmc/articles/PMC6169872/

47. When Comes A Call

101. Intercessory prayer is praying on behalf of someone else. It has been shown to be powerful. https://lifehopeandtruth.com/god/prayer-fasting-and-meditation/how-to-pray/intercessory-prayer/

102. Intercession exists in Judaism as well where it is not simply prayer, but an agreement to remain before God until the situation has been resolved. It is a commitment. https://www.jpost.com/christian-in-israel/comment/intercession-and-judaism

48. Active Faith

103. Patience, though one of the most difficult things to demonstrate, is truly a virtue. Most world religions impress upon us the power and importance of patience. https://www.psychologytoday.com/us/blog/hide-and-seek/201908/the-lost-virtue-patience

104. Instead of seeking comfort, we should strive for growth. We can accomplish much more if we seek to improve ourselves and have the courage to be uncomfortable. https://everydaypower.com/growth-over-comfort/

49. The Other Side

105. Sports, especially for young children, can be much more than simply games to play. Sports can be incredible teachers, passing on lessons and skills that will be called upon again and again throughout life. https://www.inspiresport.com/the-skills-sports-teach-us-that-we-take-into-other-areas-of-life/

106. There have been many studies done on the significance of winning and losing and how each affects a person's psychological makeup. Both are important and are crucial components to people developing into well-rounded, capable, adaptable, and resilient humans. https://www.cbsnews.com/news/the-psychology-of-winning-and-losing/

50. There is a Season

107. We all know we should take time to be still. But do we know why? https://psychcentral.com/blog/the-power-in-being-still-how-to-practice-stillness#:~:text=%E2%80%9CBeing%20still%20is%20like%20

replenishing.also%20soothes%20our%20nervous%20system.

108. We are reminded of the power of prayer, and how prayer is simply an ask for something. The King James Bible version of Matthew 7:7-8 quotes: "Ask, and it shall be given you; seek, and ye shall find; knock, and it shall be opened until you. For every one that asketh receiveth; and he that seeketh findeth; and to him that knocketh it shall be opened." https://www.biblegateway.com/passage/?search=Matthew%207%3A7-8&version=KJV

51. Righteous Among Nations

109. Oskar Schindler is reported to have saved over 1,100 Jews during the Holocaust. https://encyclopedia.ushmm.org/content/en/article/oskar-schindler

110. Chinu Sugihara, known as "a courageous diplomat of humanity" was responsible for issuing transit vitas to Japan to many Jews who were being persecuted by the Nazis. The world is full of heroes. https://www.mofa.go.jp/region/middle_e/israel/sugihara.html#:~:text=Chiune%20Sugihara%20was%20born%20on,where%20he%20earned%20high%20grades.

52. On Bended Knee

111. Another example of a life well lived is Clayton Bushnell, a World War II veteran and author of the book, *The Centurion King: The Battle for Okinawa.* https://veteransday.utah.edu/honorees/clayton-bushnell/

112. There are many ideas for what constitutes a life well lived. What is important is that we meet our own definition. https://www.psychologytoday.com/us/blog/turning-straw-gold/201508/what-is-life-well-lived

Additional Sources and Insights Supporting the Emotional and Intellectual Benefits of Poetry

1. Poetry can help with community building, literacy instruction, and self-reflection. https://study.com/learn/lesson/poetry-purpose-reasons-benefits.html

2. Poetry was hugely beneficial to many people coping with loneliness and isolation during the pandemic. https://www.ncbi.nlm.nih.gov/pmc/articles/PMC7447694/

3. Poetry can be helpful to improving our mental health, especially in times of great need. https://www.artsandmindlab.org/more-than-words-why-poetry-is-good-for-our-health/#:~:text=The%20Healing%20Word,and%20our%20place%20in%20it

4. Holding on to resentment, wrongs, and mistakes can hold us back. If we can learn to let go, we'll find the path forward to be that much easier. https://medium.com/thrive-global/the-secret-for-true-confidence-is-just-the-courage-to-let-go-1543b25a180b

5. Poetry encourages 'a certain kind of interconnectedness' which can lead to a greater understanding and healing. https://www.psychologytoday.com/intl/blog/the-empowerment-diary/201904/how-poetry-can-heal#:~:text=Writing%20poetry%20allows%20us%20to,at%20the%20moment%20of%20writing

6. Poetry, rather than prose, fosters intentionality, because words must be chosen with particular care. https://www.readpoetry.com/the-power-of-intentional-poetry/

7. Teaching poetry – in addition to prose – offers new avenues into learning outside of the traditional. https://www.theatlantic.com/education/archive/2014/04/why-teaching-poetry-is-so-important/360346/

Additional Resources Exploring the Health and Wellness Benefits of Writing Things Down and Taking Action

1. According to neuroscience, writing down our goals helps with both external storage and encoding, both things that help us work to achieve our goals. https://www.forbes.com/sites/markmurphy/2018/04/15/neuroscience-explains-why-you-need-to-write-down-your-goals-if-you-actually-want-to-achieve-them/?sh=6888d64b7905

2. Research has found that we are 42 percent more likely to accomplish a goal if we write it down. https://fullfocus.co/5-reasons-why-you-should-commit-your-goals-to-writing/

3. Writing down your goals helps you to clarify what it is that you want, and that clarity can lead to action. https://lucemiconsulting.co.uk/writing-down-your-goals/

4. Writing down your goals allows you to have better recall when you encounter the written list. Simply put: you can't ignore something you've written down as easily as something that exists only in your head. https://www.newtechnorthwest.com/the-psychology-of-writing-down-goals/

5. Personal and psychological dynamics are unlocked when we write things down. https://www.lifehack.org/385087/heres-why-writing-down-your-goals-really-does-work

6. Learn the difference between taking action and being in motion by writing down your goals. https://www.berkeleywellbeing.com/taking-action.html#:~:text=Commit%20to%20Your%20Action%20Steps,us%20stick%20to%20doing%20it.

7. Taking action can be a difficult thing. This piece gives tips for moving beyond making a decision and taking action. https://www.skipprichard.com/the-action-habit-7-proven-ways-to-move-from-deciding-to-doing/

Additional Sources Concerning Letting Go and the Power of Forgiveness for Health and Well-Being

1. In order to forgive, we must possess the courage and let go of the cosmic scale balancing. https://ancientchristianwisdom.wordpress.com/2014/07/08/forgiveness-requires-courage/

2. Forgiving is a verb; it must be done actively and with intent. Choosing to forgive is a powerful action. https://www.churchofjesuschrist.org/study/ensign/2014/01/choosing-to-forgive?lang=eng

3. The act of forgiveness and making it part of your life can have health benefits in terms of improved immune response and how your body deals with stress. https://www.hopkinsmedicine.org/health/wellness-and-prevention/forgiveness-your-health-depends-on-it

4. Practicing forgiveness regularly can lead to 'lower levels of depression, anxiety, and hostility; reduced substance abuse; higher self-esteem; and greater life satisfaction.'" https://www.health.harvard.edu/mind-and-mood/the-power-of-forgiveness#:~:text=Practicing%20forgiveness%20can%20have%20powerful,esteem%3B%20and%20greater%20life%20satisfaction

5. If you can learn to be self-reflective, you will learn a great deal about yourself, which can help you work better and be more compassionate with others. https://hbr.org/2022/03/dont-underestimate-the-power-of-self-reflection

6. By focusing on the past, we lose sight of who we are in the present. Letting go allows us to move forward. https://www.mindful.org/what-it-means-to-let-go-and-why-its-an-essential-part-of-healing/

7. There are a variety of ways to go about moving on, many involve asking yourself where the pain lives, and if it's something you can continue to carry. https://psychcentral.com/blog/how-to-let-go-of-the-past-and-hurt

Additional Sources Regarding the Importance of Expressing Love and Gratitude

1. Practicing gratitude regularly can help our physical and mental well-being. https://iyde.org/blog/the-importance-of-gratitude-on-your-well-being/?gclid=CjwKCAjwgsqoBhBNEiwAwe5w0_7v67SaeFcN5Z2khmfbThRjEfeZQNQYCGPVXDHwKhgjv7as1r49YhoCJDQQAvD_BwE

2. Gratitude leads to positive emotions, which can improve your health and relationships. https://www.health.harvard.edu/healthbeat/giving-thanks-can-make-you-happier#:~:text=Gratitude%20helps%20people%20feel%20more,express%20gratitude%20in%20multiple%20ways.

3. This article gives examples of exercises in gratitude we can perform to improve our outlook and as part of self-care. https://positivepsychology.com/gratitude-appreciation/

4. Practicing gratitude encourages mindfulness, an important component of balanced mental well-being. https://www.helpguide.org/articles/mental-health/gratitude.htm

5. Gratitude allows for an open appreciation of one's community, which encourages strong relationships. https://www.forbes.com/sites/tracybrower/2021/01/03/gratitude-is-good-why-its-important-and-how-to-cultivate-it/?sh=5f9e283d2a0f

6. Research has shown – and continues to show – that gratitude can "heal, energize, and change lives." https://www.nytimes.com/2023/06/08/well/mind/gratitude-health-benefits.html

7. Behavior can change our biology. Practicing gratitude and outward expressions of appreciation can actually make us happier and healthier. https://www.mayoclinichealthsystem.org/hometown-health/speaking-of-health/can-expressing-gratitude-improve-health

K.S. DWYER IS THE AUTHOR OF THE PEARL SERIES AND MANY OTHER WORKS.

Pearls for Prosperity

A treasure map for success, peace and genuine living, Pearls for Prosperity takes you on a journey of self discovery and generosity. Chart your own course to prosperity with this rousing adventure.

Poetry for Peace

K.S. Dwyer presents a collection of inspirational poems about life's experiences-both the everyday and the extraordinary - and how one's perspective can encourage wholeness and peace.

LEARN MORE AT:

www.ksdwyer.com

www.ingramcontent.com/pod-product-compliance
Lightning Source LLC
Chambersburg PA
CBHW021516110225
21522CB00004B/102